MW01240859

Body Dysmorphia (BDD)

The Holistic Approach to Take Control of Your Obsessive Negative Thoughts, Stop Comparing and Learn to Love Your Appearance. Enhance Professional Help and Therapy

Caldwell Ramsey

© *Copyright 2023 -All rights reserved.*

The contents of this book may not be reproduced, duplicated or transmitted without direct written permission from the author. Under no circumstances will any legal responsibility or blame be held against the publisher for any reparation, damages, or monetary loss due to the information herein, either directly or indirectly.

Legal Notice:

This book is copyright protected. This is only for personal use. You cannot amend, distribute, sell, use, quote or paraphrase any part or the content within this book without the consent of the author.

Disclaimer Notice:

Please note the information contained within this document is for educational and entertainment purposes only. Every attempt has been made to provide accurate, up to date and reliable complete information. No warranties of any kind are expressed or implied. Readers acknowledge that the author is not engaging in the rendering of legal, financial, medical or professional advice. The content of this book has been derived from various sources. Please consult a licensed professional before attempting any techniques outlined in this book.

By reading this document, the reader agrees that under no circumstances is the author responsible for any losses, direct or indirect, which are incurred as a result of the use of information contained within this document, including, but not limited to,

—errors, omissions, or inaccuracies.

ISBN Number - 9798398136029

This book is dedicated to all the beautiful humans suffering from body image issues, you are not alone and you are not your body. You are a gift to the world, made exactly as you were meant to be, you are perfectly imperfect. I wish you inner peace, self-love and happiness.

-C. Ramsey

Table of Contents

Just For You

A Free Gift For All My Readers

BDD - Body Love Workbook
with complementary tools for your healing
journey. Visit my website:

www.CaldwellRamseybooks.com

Introduction

"I'd rather risk death than look like this for the rest of my life."

That is the decision I made when I opted for plastic surgery to 'fix' what I hated most about my appearance. Imagine how shocked I was when, even after surgery, I was still not happy. I still hated how I looked. What could be wrong with me that even a surgeon's knife couldn't fix how I look? I didn't know that the problem wasn't how I looked; it was how I felt about how I looked.

Body dysmorphia has been around since the dawn of time, we have simply never given it a name. During the past century, thanks to online articles, magazines, and books written by people who have experienced body dysmorphia and body dysmorphic disorder (BDD), we are now aware of the true effect it has on us physically, mentally, and spiritually.

This book is written specifically for those who suspect they need help but are not sure of the next step to take. As it is a sensitive subject and not much talked about in social circles, the aim of this book is to teach you to help yourself and, if needed, seek professional help.

This book teaches how the disorder affects our daily lives and the lives of people in our circle—colleagues, friends, and family. It includes ways of analyzing the functions of the brain that contribute to this issue, and it will enlighten you to start working on your life in an authentic, loving, and accepting manner through holistic living.

The goal of this book is to share key learnings and coping methods from someone who understands this disorder from personal experience. That someone is me, Caldwell Ramsey.

I feel strongly that there is not enough supportive literature aimed at helping people recognize BDD. The literature that is available is written more by academics and researchers who either don't understand the reality of living with BDD or don't write about it in such a way that everyday people can relate.

Living with BDD

We are born self-critical. These critical thoughts could be worsened by life events. The sad reality is that for generations, society has favored what they perceive as perfect, and today, social media promotes an almost inaccessible standard of perfection.

The images we see in magazines, on posters, and all over the internet – including our personal social media feeds – are often not real. Filters and Photoshop add a level of fake not easily discernible with the naked eye. The stark reality is, our brains can't tell if it's fake, so our minds assume it's real. This exacerbates the downward spiral of not being able to 'keep up', so we lapse into self-loathing.

Pause for a moment and realize that you are a unique individual with unique talents. You were created for a special purpose. Learn to love the skin you are in and consider the magnificence of how you were naturally formed – perfect for your unique talents.

Understanding the Underlying Conditions

After years of searching for answers and undergoing a few cosmetic surgeries (yet still not feeling happy and content), I realized that understanding the underlying issues and finding a solution that considered body, mind, and spirit would be the only way to find lasting inner peace.

I chose holistic healing, an option that covers all aspects of life—aspects that work together to form a wholly unique and happy human being, able to interact with others naturally, recognizing that everyone has body dysmorphic issues about some part of their body.

In creating a new mindset filled with love and acceptance, I opted for techniques that included self-love, self-compassion, feelings of self-worthiness, and living life authentically. That also included living in the present moment and finding love and peace by practicing healthier thoughts and actions.

Living holistically means finding contentment in one's body image, feeling emotionally connected, and learning to pivot negative thoughts into happy, positive, and grateful ones. Holistic living brings about a space where natural healing can occur with the support of loving-kindness, gratitude, purpose, and worthiness.

I suffered from BDD, although not officially diagnosed, negative thoughts about my body image made my life unbearable. These thoughts and insecurities prompted me to seek help in the cosmetic surgery fraternity. Unfortunately, the surgeons fueled my already prevalent insecurities.

Eventually I realized that delving deeper into self-reflection and personal psyche would provide the help that outsiders never could.

Understanding and overcoming BDD to live a full and happy life became a quest. Once I realized there was joy beyond pain, I knew I had to inspire others to look beyond the ever-present BDD reality to the hope of a life without it.

By changing my thought patterns, I changed my life situation. Now, I want to inspire others through my journey.

This book is written with the wish that all who read it will know where to start the inner healing process and develop self-compassion and acceptance in this challenging journey of life. More than this, it is a book that opens a gateway of possibilities to mindful living and healing.

The focus of this book is to not be caught up in a bubble of BDD but to burst the bubble and explode into a full life!

This book is the first step in acknowledging that you have body dysmorphia or possibly body dysmorphic disorder. It will give you the tools to minimize the symptoms and hurt. If, after reading this book, you feel you need professional help, find a licensed professional who will work with you and understand that you have done your research but require additional help.

Chapter 1

Body Dysmorphic Disorder (BDD)

"Stop spending all day obsessing, cursing, perfecting your body like it's all you've got to offer the world. Your body is not your art, it's your paintbrush."

—Glennon Doyle

As the saying goes, we first need to know the nature of the beast before we conquer it.

That's why I decided to start this book and hopefully your healing journey by explaining to you exactly what body dysmorphic disorder is, how it can affect your life, and how to know whether you are likely to have it.

Taking this first step was exactly how I began to admit that, yes, my therapist friend was right when he took me aside one day and suggested that I could have BDD.

With the information I gathered over many hours, weeks, months, and years, I understood that I wasn't alone in how I felt about my body and that there was hope. I could create the right environment and mentality I needed to love myself, take control of my thoughts and create the happy life that I deserved.

Living in this modern society where we're faced with images of so-called body perfection is not easy.

I only had to pick up my phone and scroll through Facebook or Instagram to be confronted with everything that I wasn't and find myself slipping down into that dark hole of anxiety, self-doubt, and insecurity. I'm not alone in this.

Body image issues alone affect as many as 50% of the population because we feel under so much pressure to look good. Real people don't look like the images we see in the media, so it's no wonder that many of us struggle.

However, there's a big difference between feeling insecure about the way we look or having body image issues and suffering from BDD.

Body Dysmorphic Disorder is a mental health problem where we can't control the negative thoughts we have about our appearance. We don't believe people when they tell us that we are fine and experience severe emotional distress that can interfere with our daily lives.

At one point, my experience of BDD became so bad that I ended my relationship with the person I was engaged to. All that overthinking and self-hate impacted our relationship significantly and there was no way we could continue together. I didn't feel good enough, nor that I would ever be. I let my problems become greater than my relationship, which completely ruined what we had. After the breakup, I was alone and in a much worse place in my thoughts. I felt like a freak.

But as I continued my research into BDD, I soon discovered that I wasn't alone. The disorder is thought to affect between 1.4 to 2.4% of the global population[1], with many more undiagnosed and struggling to live their lives under this painful dictator…

Whether you have been formally diagnosed by a medical practitioner or haven't yet looked for help, I want you to know that there is light at the end of the tunnel. You, too, can come through this difficult period in your life, take control of your negative thoughts and learn to live a rich, vibrant, and happy life.

Join me as I guide you through the first stage of your healing journey and help you understand exactly what you are experiencing.

What exactly is Body Dysmorphic Disorder?

Body dysmorphic disorder is a mental health problem that leaves us believing that there are significant flaws in our appearance.

---

[1]   Cleveland Clinic. (n.d.). Body dysmorphic disorder (BDD): Symptoms & treatment. Cleveland Clinic. Retrieved March 4, 2023, from https://my.cleve-landclinic.org/health/diseases/9888-body-dysmorphic-disorder#

We spend hours in front of the mirror, inspecting every inch of our bodies and harshly criticizing ourselves about some aspect of it, even if it's unnoticeable to others or totally insignificant.

For me, this mainly manifested as an obsession with the shape of my body. Every time I passed a mirror, I was given a harsh and traumatic reminder of how ugly and worthless I was. To my eyes, my body was disproportioned. It was all the proof I needed that I was flawed as a human being.

If I wanted to be accepted by society, not ridiculed, and especially, deserving of love, I had to conceal this terrible flaw of mine until I could fix it. Making peace with it was not an option. So, I dressed in clothes that hid my body, exercised, counted calories, lifted weights, avoided full-body mirrors, and refused to pose for photos. If my partner and I did anything fun and wanted to capture the moment with a photo, it had to be a head-and-shoulders shot. No one on social media was allowed to discover this devastating imperfection in my body.

I turned to the surgeon's knife and underwent two cosmetic surgeries to fix what I did not like about my body. But in spite of that, I wasn't happy. I still hated what I saw in the mirror.

To be honest, this left me in a desperate state. If even surgery didn't fix me, what was I supposed to do? Continue to hide under layers of clothing? Avoid mirrors and cameras forever? Undergo further expensive surgery that I really couldn't afford? Resign myself to the undeniable fact that I was ugly and unlovable?

I'll admit that I did spiral into a deep hole of self-hate and negativity at this point. I stopped listening to my friend's completely **because** I knew they were liars… they were just too scared to admit that they thought I had a freakish body.

I stayed at home often, feeling safe from the judgmental eyes of the outside world but still suffering painfully inside. Even if I covered up the mirrors in my home, I knew that my misshapen body was still there. Evidence of the fact that I was deeply flawed as a human being.

Those long hours at home caused my brain to spiral even more. I found myself thinking that my friends, my family, and the world would be better off without me. No, I didn't exactly consider ending it all, but I did want it to stop. I just wanted to find some relief from the relentless, exhausting, torturous existence that every day had become.

If you're reading this book, you can most likely relate to my experience, even if it's not your body you hate. Perhaps you believe that your skin is ugly or blemished, your lips are too thin or too thick, or your ears, chin, genitals, or breasts lack symmetry, are out of proportion, or are plain hideous and revolting.

Like me, you spend hours obsessing about how you look, often checking how bad your flaw looks, camouflaging it, altering it, or avoiding social situations or triggers that can increase your distress.

What is key here is the fact that there isn't anything intrinsically wrong with how you look. It's your perception. Others most likely don't even notice your self-perceived flaw or find it so insignificant because they love you for exactly who you are.

But this doesn't help if you have BDD. You are fixated on this flaw and believe that everything will be perfect once the defect is fixed. Then you could have total control over your life and finally, feel confident and happy.

Do you have BDD? The Symptoms

Many people aren't entirely happy with one of their features and would prefer that their skin was better, their hair was thicker, or that their bodies were differently shaped. But this doesn't interfere too much with their happiness, self-esteem, or confidence.

But for those like us with BDD, our obsession with our appearance can become traumatic and life-changing and prevent us from living the amazing lives we deserve.

If you have any of the following symptoms, you could have BDD.

- You constantly check yourself in the mirror or avoid mirrors altogether.

- You try to hide the body part you dislike with a hat, scarf, clothes, or makeup.

- You are constantly negatively comparing yourself to others.

- You frequently ask other people if you look OK (and don't believe them when they say you look fine).

- You exercise or groom yourself excessively.

- You frequently change your clothes.

- You avoid social activities or leaving the house.

- You dislike bright light or leaving the house during the daytime.

- You believe that other people judge your appearance or mock you.

- You pick at your skin with your fingers or tweezers.

- You've seen many healthcare providers about your perceived flaw.

- Your feelings about your appearance have a significant impact on your quality of life.

- You feel anxious, depressed, ashamed, or have considered suicide.

- You suffer from other mental health disorders, social anxiety, depression, eating disorders, or OCD.

- As I mentioned earlier, the key difference is that BDD is a mental health problem with severe consequences, not just a dislike for one part of your body.

Body Dysmorphic Disorder: Self-Assessment Quiz

If you haven't yet been diagnosed and would like to understand whether you could have the disorder or want to understand how severe your symptoms are, work through the following quiz and write your answers down somewhere, such as in a journal. This way, you can use your answers for future reference and to see how far in your healing journey you have come.

I'd also like to add that you MUST be completely honest when you're answering these questions. Many sufferers deny that they have a problem or minimize the effect that it's having on their lives because they're afraid of what this could mean. Please don't fall into this trap. This quiz was designed for your eyes only, and by being honest, you are more likely to find the most effective paths toward healing.

Note that this is for self-assessment purposes only and isn't meant to serve as a diagnosis.

Body Dysmorphia (BDD)

1. How often do you check your appearance in a mirror, a window, or by checking it with your fingers?

- 40 times or more per day

- 20 times or more per day

- 10 times or more per day

- 5 times or more per day

- Never

2. How ugly or unattractive do you believe your features are?

- Very ugly

- Extremely unattractive

- Moderately unattractive

- Slightly unattractive

- Not unattractive

3. How much distress do you feel because of your features?

- Not distressing

- Slightly distressing

- Moderately distressing

- Markedly distressing

- Extremely distressing

4. Do you ever avoid situations or activities because of your appearance? If so, how often?

- Always

- About 75% of the time

- About 50% of the time

- About 25% of the time

- Never

5. How much do your features preoccupy you?

- Not at all

- Slightly

- Moderately

- Very much

- Extremely

6. Do your features affect your relationship with a partner (if you have one) or affect your dating life?

- Not at all

- Slightly

- Moderately

- Very much

- Extremely

7. Do your features interfere with your ability to work or study?

- Not at all

- Slightly

- Moderately

- Markedly

- Very seriously

8. Do your features interfere with your social life?

- Not at all

- Slightly

- Moderately

- Markedly

- Very seriously

9. Do you believe that your appearance is the most important part of who you are as a person? If so, to what extent?

- Not at all

- Slightly

- Moderately

- Mostly

- Totally

- Very seriously

*Adapted from the Body Dysmorphic Disorder Foundation website[2]. Visit their website for further information.

What type of BDD do you have?

More likely than not, you fall into the main type of body dysmorphic disorder, as I shared above. However, there are also two main subtypes of BDD[3]: muscle dysmorphia and BDD by proxy, which can also have a significant impact on your life. Read through the list of symptoms of each of these below and see if you can relate.

Muscle Dysmorphia (MD)

Muscle dysmorphia (also nicknamed 'reverse anorexia') is a subtype of BDD where you believe that your body isn't muscular or large enough. You might find yourself using dangerous substances such as anabolic steroids to bulk up, focus excessively on your diet and spend many hours at the gym or exercising.

You might also:

- Overvalue your appearance and believe that people judge you for it.

- Suffer from intrusive thoughts about your body.

- Repeatedly count calories or balance carbs, fats, proteins, and vitamins.

- Avoid certain social situations where your body could be on display (such as the beach or swimming pool).

- Avoid eating at restaurants because of a perceived lack of control over your food.

[2] Veale, D., Ellison, N., Werner, T., Dodhia, R., Serfaty, M., & Clarke, A. (n.d.). Do I have BDD? Take the test. BDDF. Retrieved March 3, 2023, from https://bddfoundation.org/information/do-i-have-bdd-test/

[3] OCD Foundation. (n.d.). Subtypes of BDD. BDD. Retrieved March 3, 2023, from https://bdd.iocdf.org/about-bdd/subtypes-of-bdd/

- Work out or lift weights for many hours per day.

- Camouflage your body by wearing multiple layers of clothes so you look larger.

If you're a bodybuilder, fitness fanatic, and/or practice endurance sports like ultrarunning, you could have this type of BDD but deny that there is a problem and refuse help. The problem then only worsens, affecting your overall health significantly.

Body Dysmorphic Disorder by Proxy

Unlike many other types of BDD, BDD by Proxy (BDDBP) is an obsession with another person's appearance and not your own. This person is known as a 'person of concern' or POC and is usually a spouse or partner but can equally be a parent, child, sibling, or even a complete stranger. It can also shift over time between people.

While this may seem strange, your concern causes the same distress and interferes with your ability to function normally in the world. You could even spend hours a day thinking about these perceived defects. Usually, this is focused on one body area but most often concerns the person's hair or skin.

If you suffer from BDDBP, you may:

- Perform repetitive behaviors to ease your anxiety.

- Try to improve the POC's appearance (by checking or hiding a certain feature or comparing their appearance to others).

- Avoid social situations where the POC's flaw will be visible.

- Believe that people stare or laugh at the POC's appearance.

- Feel shame or guilt about your preoccupation.

- Worry that BDD will damage your relationship with that person.

Before we go any further, take a few moments to consider which type of BDD you may have, bearing in mind that you could have a combination of two types. Note this down with the quiz you worked through earlier and keep your findings somewhere safe.

With this information, you can better understand what you are experiencing and find the right treatment to meet your needs, whether this is by following the advice in this book or by seeking the help of a professional.

How does BDD affect your life?

If you're reading this book, you've already felt the effects that BDD can have on your life. It can be overwhelming, painful, torturous, and leave you feeling extremely anxious and desperate for relief.

Having said that, many of us downplay just how severe the problem can be and the impact it's having on our lives. We don't want to admit to our vulnerabilities or show any weaknesses, let alone ask for help.

However, if you want to break free from this toxic cycle of anxiety and rediscover the self-esteem, confidence, and happiness that you deserve, you must take the same difficult step that I did and admit to yourself how you're really feeling.

Yes, I know it can be hard. Even though I knew that I had a problem, and I was desperate to find relief, I continued to deny the true extent of my experience of BDD. In some crazy way, my preoccupation with my appearance helped me feel I was in control of my life. Admitting that I needed help or dropping my obsessive thoughts felt like jumping headfirst off a cliff blindfolded, crossing my fingers, and hoping that there was a net to catch me.

But there WAS a net. What I didn't realize at the time was that there was a net to catch me.

It was my own immense desire to heal and move through this difficult period in my life. I knew it wouldn't be easy. I also knew that I'd need to face some of my demons along the way.

But I needed to find my 'why'. I needed to understand that the disorder was controlling me and not keeping me safe! Only then would I find the strength to break free from the shackles and fly free.

You, too, can do this. Find a quiet space where you can relax, grab a pen and a journal, and come with me as we take time to consider what effect BDD is having on your life. Ready? Let's get started.

Take five minutes to answer each of these groups of questions and write them down in your book.

Q1. Your mood

- How do you feel on an average day?

- Do you suffer from anxiety, sadness, or a low mood?

- Do you feel disgusted with yourself?

- Do you have less energy than you had before?

- Do you suffer from eating or sleeping problems?

- Do you struggle to concentrate?

- Do you find it hard to enjoy the things you did before?

- Do you feel depressed?

- Have you ever considered suicide?

Q2. Your social life

- Do you ever want to hide your appearance from others?

- Do you find it difficult to make eye contact, speak or interact with others?

- Do you feel self-conscious in social situations?

- Have you given up the activities you love?

- Do you feel lonely or socially isolated?

- Do you feel that you don't deserve friends or social contact?

- Have you stopped enjoying time spent with other people?

- Do you avoid having a boyfriend or girlfriend?

- Do you avoid having sex?

- Do you avoid leaving the house (especially during daylight hours) because of how you feel about your appearance?

Q3. *Family life and relationships*

- Have your relationships with family, friends, or loved ones suffered because of BDD?

- Do you frequently seek reassurance about your appearance from family, friends, or loved ones?

- Have those closest to you ever expressed their concern about BDD or encouraged you to seek help? If so, how did you react?

- Have you lost friends or romantic partners because of BDD?

- Do you ever have arguments with others because of BDD?

- Do your loved ones try to frequently reassure you about your appearance?

- Do you cancel plans to avoid leaving the house?

- Do you feel different from other people?

- Do you avoid making friends or dating because you're afraid of being judged or rejected?

Q4. *Problems at work or school*

- Has your performance at school or work suffered because of BDD?

- Do you avoid important meetings, presentations, or interactions with your peers or staff because of how you feel about your body?

- Have you ever missed school or work because of BDD?

- Do you find it hard to concentrate on work or school?

- Do you avoid work outings, team-building exercises, or extra-curricular activities?

- Do you feel isolated and alone at work or school?

Q5. Lifestyle habits

- Do you drink or use recreational drugs to feel better?

- Do you take anabolic steroids or performance enhancers?

- Do you go to the gym excessively or exercise obsessively?

- Do you avoid eating out at restaurants or at other people's homes because of your strict dietary requirements?

- Do you count calories or feel overly concerned about your macronutrient balance?

Q6. Financial strain

- Are you suffering from financial problems because of BDD?

- Have you paid large amounts of money for cosmetic surgery or dermatology treatment?

- Have you left employment because of your symptoms?

- Are you in debt because of loans or credit card payments to pay for your treatments?

If you've skipped through this section because you're keen to start the healing process, please stop and go back through these questions in turn, taking time to write them down. Your ability to heal and enjoy a vibrant, confident, and healthy life could depend on it!

What causes Body Dysmorphic Disorder?

It's natural to want to understand exactly why we developed BDD in the first place. I certainly found myself pouring over my past, wondering if that critical comment from an ex-partner triggered my anxiety. Or if I got unlucky when it came to the genetic lottery and inherited this disorder from my family…

To be quite honest, although it did help shed light on how I was feeling, it didn't help me to address the problem. In fact, it added fuel to my obsessive thought patterns.

But it did help me realize one very important fact—my body dysmorphic disorder wasn't my fault.

That's why I've decided to add a quick overview of some of the reasons why we can develop BDD, including some of the science behind what is happening in our brains to leave us feeling like this.

In a nutshell, BDD often arises due to a combination of environmental, psychological, or biological (genetic) factors, as with other mental health disorders.

This can include:

- Experiencing abuse, trauma, bullying, or other difficult life circumstances.

- A family history of BDD or mental health disorders.

- Personality type.

- Abnormal levels of brain chemicals such as serotonin.

- A personal history of other mental health problems such as schizophrenia, OCD, or anorexia.

- Insufficient levels of brain chemicals like serotonin and oxytocin.

What's going on in your brain?

Scientists have carried out various research studies[4] to understand what is happening in the brain of a BDD sufferer so they can develop more effective treatments. While much of this needs further exploration, they have discovered several interesting facts that I wanted to share with you before we continue.

Your serotonin levels are disrupted with BDD

Research has discovered that those with BDD often have abnormal levels of serotonin[3]. This hormone carries messages between the nerve cells in your brain and body and plays a role in your mood, sleep, digestion, and sexual desire, to name just a few. This is why antidepressants can often help reduce symptoms, ease emotional distress, and reduce depression or suicidal thinking.

Your oxytocin levels are likely to be abnormally high

Oxytocin is often known as 'the cuddle hormone' or 'love hormone' because it's involved with the human bonding process. When a parent cuddles their child or their partner, this feel-good hormone is released. In one study[3], scientists found that oxytocin levels were higher in the brains of BDD sufferers, and more interesting of all, the higher the levels, the more severe the symptoms. There are several theories of why this happens. Some suggest that these elevated levels are our body's attempts to compensate for the lack of social contact or part of our body's stress response. Although more research is clearly needed in this area, fixing brain chemistry appears to help ease symptoms.

Your thinking powers are inhibited with BDD

Scientists have also noted that memory, decision-making, and emotional processing also play a role in BDD[3]. In certain studies, individuals with the disorder struggled with impaired visual, auditory, verbal, and local memory. Interestingly, they also excelled in recalling the specific details of a certain scenario but struggled with the overall 'bigger picture'.

---

[4] Deshpande, R., Lai, T. M., Li, W., & Feusner, J. (n.d.). The neurobiology of body dysmorphic disorder. BDD. Retrieved March 3, 2023, from https://bdd.iocdf.org/professionals/neurobiology-of-bdd/

Those with BDD also appear to struggle with decision-making and perform poorly when it comes to planning, organization, search tasks, and inhibition. This could be the result of the disrupted brain chemicals (as mentioned above), and the effect that the stress of BDD can have on a person's brain and body.

You find it harder to perceive emotions accurately

With BDD, it's harder for us to recognize facial expressions, and we're more likely to identify neutral faces as angry or disgusted. We also find it harder to understand facial expressions overall and have a delayed response when it comes to positive words like 'beauty' or 'attractive' compared with neutral words. We're also more likely to see a threat in an ambiguous situation and have poor insight into our illness. Again, this could be a combination of abnormal hormone levels alongside traumatic life experiences.

Your brain structure is different

Studies of both men and women with BDD[3] have shown that the structure of our brains is different from those without the disorder.

We appear to have more white grey matter (the part that transmits signals across our brains), less grey matter (where most of our brain cells are located), abnormal symmetry deep in our brains, and changes in our overall brain volume and thickness. When we are shown faces, bodies, and houses, our brains also demonstrate abnormal activity.

So what exactly does that mean for us? Again, it's hard to define what is the cause of the problem and what is simply an effect. Having said that, factors like abnormal brain development, environmental circumstances, our thought patterns, and our life circumstances could all play a role.

It's not your fault

As you can see from reading some of these scientific facts, there's nothing that you've done to cause BDD.

This is really important for me to emphasize because I spent many years believing that I was to blame for it all. Somehow, it was my fault that I was born with this 'flaw', and it was my fault that I felt so broken because of it. I was ugly, flawed, bad at relationships, undeserving of love, and had no value as a human being.

But from reading the scientific research, I soon came to understand two key facts:

1. I wasn't to blame for how I was feeling. Whatever had caused me to spiral into this dark and traumatic place was to blame, NOT ME.

2. I could do something about it. I wasn't powerless. I wasn't a victim. I could break free of the clutches of BDD and rediscover a happy, healthy, and fulfilling life.

Getting treatment for BDD

The very fact that you have this book in your hands shows that you want help changing the way you think and feel about yourself and how you behave. You are no longer willing to accept feeling bad or living a meaningless life and want to break out of your mental prison and feel happy and fulfilled.

By reading this book, you've taken that first step toward healing.

But I know all too well what might happen next. If you're anything like me, you'll read and absorb the information I'm sharing and maybe even work through the prompts, determined to get better. Then somehow, you end up getting lost on the way. It just feels too scary, traumatic, and difficult to face your problems, let alone get the treatment you need. Or something causes you to relapse, and you are unable to see light at the end of the tunnel at all…

You lose your momentum, your desire, and your sense of personal strength and find yourself trapped by ever-worsening symptoms and obsessive thoughts.

So, before we head into the next chapter and start the healing process, I want to encourage you to get the treatment you need before it's too late. I've seen far too many lives crumble and, due to my struggle with the disorder, lost too many friends. I'm not willing to stand by and let more people suffer.

The truth is, if you don't get the treatment you need, you can suffer from serious side effects, like depression. A startling statistic reveals that there is a high rate of suicide among BDD sufferers—some studies suggest this figure could be as high as 25%.[5]

I was one of the lucky ones in my support network (more on that later) who broke free and reclaimed their lives, and I want you to do the same. Together we can get through this.

---

[5] BDD Foundation. (n.d.). Feeling suicidal? BDDF. Retrieved March 3, 2023, from https://bddfoundation.org/support/feeling-suicidal/

Remember that this book isn't a replacement for professional help but a path towards understanding the challenges you face and discovering which holistic methods you can use to enhance and use alongside any professional help. Please reach out to a licensed medical professional if you believe you have BDD.

Summary

In this chapter, we've started to explore BDD and understand what it is, what the symptoms are, how it can affect your life and what can trigger or cause it.

I also gave you two self-assessment quizzes to help you identify if it really is BDD and to understand your experience of the disorder. If you haven't done these quizzes yet, I highly recommend that you go back and do them, then keep your results somewhere safe. You can then use these to track how far you are in your healing journey and identify what else you need to work on.

Chapter 2

Understanding BDD

"Awareness is the first step in healing."

- Dean Ornish

We kickstarted this book by exploring some of the facts about what BDD actually is, the symptoms, and what can cause it. Then we spent some time thinking about whether you could have the disorder, got clear on what symptoms you are experiencing, and how it's currently affecting your life.

I took exactly these same steps when I started my healing journey so I could overcome one of the biggest obstacles—that I did indeed have body dysmorphia disorder and, perhaps, more importantly, that I wasn't broken or a freak. There were millions of people out there just like me who felt the same mental torment and had their lives totally controlled by BDD.

But there was one thing that was missing. None of this information helped me to understand myself better, learn what the potential causes or triggers of my unique experience could be, and help me find my own path through.

I knew that if I didn't rebuild, it would be like launching an arrow into the darkness. Sure, it might somehow hit the target and help me. But more likely than not, it would miss entirely, and I wouldn't be able to heal.

That was a risk I wasn't willing to take. So I took matters into my own hands and dedicated many hours, days, and weeks to self-reflection, picking apart those childhood experiences, adult encounters, and other potential triggers that had led me to this dark and traumatic place.

In this chapter, I'll be taking you by the hand and guiding you through this self-reflection process. You'll finally understand that BDD isn't your fault but a mental illness that can happen to anyone, regardless of their intelligence, race, background, financial status, or culture.

With the help of the information and self-reflection exercises I've included, you'll understand yourself even better and start to develop a framework for your healing journey. It may not be easy, especially if you need to revisit those childhood bullying experiences or think back to how you were raised. But I promise you that by doing this, you'll be taking this first step, however tiny, into recovery.

So, who gets BDD?

Until just a few years ago, people thought that BDD was extremely rare. But the truth is, it's more common than we thought. Recent statistics suggest that anywhere between 5-10 million Americans are currently struggling with its vicious grip. This figure could even be higher because people with BDD are less likely to speak to friends, family members, doctors, and therapists about their feelings because they're embarrassed, ashamed, and, quite often, misunderstood. For example, my ex-partner was convinced that I was vain or self-obsessed because I used to check myself in the mirror so frequently. They thought that I was completely engrossed with my appearance and that the issue was an overinflated ego, not a mental health disorder.

This couldn't have been further from the truth. I felt so ugly—broken inside and beyond repair. Besides, what would they do with me if I did seek help or treatment? Laugh in my face and send me home to continue my struggles? Expose my greatest weaknesses and vulnerabilities and make me feel even worse than I already did?

While I felt like this, I was letting those negative thoughts and compulsive behaviors control my life, not the other way around. I also didn't realize that there was a huge amount of help available to me if only I'd taken a deep breath, admitted to the problem, and reached out for help.

I wish I'd known at the time that I wasn't a freak, and I certainly wasn't alone. Both men and women all over the world can develop BDD.

A few world-renowned celebrities are thought to have suffered from BDD, which had a devastating effect on their lives and, in some cases, led to their early deaths.[6]

---

[6]   BDD Foundation . (n.d.). Famous people with BDD. BDDF. Retrieved March 13, 2023, from https://bddfoundation.org/information/more-about-bdd/famous-people-with-bdd/

Why do we feel like this?

Life is complex. Mental health is complex. That's why it can be so difficult to pinpoint exactly why we develop BDD and what continues to feed this disorder.

As I mentioned in the previous chapter, it is usually a combination of your life experiences, personality type, overall risk of mental health disorders, an imbalance of brain chemicals, and genetic factors.

Does this information help you at all? I'm guessing not. The problem is, it's too vague and doesn't help us to understand exactly what is going on with our experience of BDD or how to overcome it.

Another problem is that the medical profession often can't pinpoint exactly what causes the problem itself.

Are those low serotonin levels to blame for your symptoms, or are they actually *caused* by BDD? Is your DNA and the fact that you have a family history of mental health problems the underlying cause, or is it that their experiences affected the way you were raised, your attachment style, or the way you see the world?

Let me give you a personal example to explain what I mean. My mother suffered from severe anxiety throughout her life, in part due to a difficult childhood. I remember her suffering from severe bouts of depression during my childhood and teenage years which obviously affected me significantly.

Does that mean that it played a role in my developing BDD? Does the fact that we share the same DNA mean that I, too, was more likely to suffer from anxiety or depression? Or was it just that this traumatic experience during my most vulnerable years left its mark?

BDD isn't your fault

Whatever the causes may be, it's important to remember that your experience of BDD has been triggered by something. Again, it's not your fault or something intrinsic but something that has happened to you.

Psychologists place BDD on the OCD (obsessive compulsive disorder) spectrum because of the severe obsessive thoughts we experience and the effect these thoughts have on our lives. It's also based on fear, the desire to control how we are feeling, and the need to protect ourselves from the world—to control rather than to be controlled. But that's where the irony is.

Let's think back to our caveman days.[7] We lived very harsh lives and were constantly faced with predators who could kill us and our families.

Nature helped ensure the survival of our species with the so-called 'fight or flight' response. When faced with a hungry tiger looking for its next meal, we'd either flee or fight back to keep ourselves and our loved ones alive. Then, we'd use our human superpower of being able to imagine a hypothetical future and almost certainly take steps to make sure it didn't happen again. Maybe we'd take weapons, remain hidden, or simply avoid going to that place again.

A similar process happens with BDD. For whatever reason, something triggered a stress response in you (more on that in a second), and now your body and mind are trying to protect you from any potential threat.

The only problem with BDD is that once the traumatic event happens and we take action to protect ourselves (by checking the mirror, avoiding certain scenarios, or even undergoing cosmetic surgery), we *still* don't feel any relief. We *still* feel unsafe. The world *still* feels like a scary and intimidating place. Our symptoms can often become worse unless we break the cycle and seek help.

What could have triggered BDD?

Often the BDD stress response happens as a result of a traumatic life experience. If you have certain personality traits or a history of mental health disorders, this is likely to make the problem even worse.

When you think back through your past, do you remember anything that could be partly responsible? If not, don't worry—we'll be doing more self-reflection shortly to help you make sense of your own experience of BDD so you can start on your path toward healing.

---

[7] Abed, R. T. (n.d.). An Evolutionary Hypothesis For Obsessive Compulsive Disorder: A Psychological Immune System? An evolutionary hypothesis for obsessive compulsive disorder: A psychological immune system? Retrieved March 13, 2023, from https://web-archive.southampton.ac.uk/cog-prints.org/1147/1/ocd-final.htm

In the meantime, I'd like to share with you some of the possible triggers.[8] As you read through, consider whether you can relate. If so, make a note of them and keep it somewhere safe—we'll be coming back to it later.

Abuse or bullying

Often, a traumatic experience in your past can increase your risk of developing BDD.[9] This can include abuse or neglect as a child, poor attachment, bullying as a teenager, or rejection from your caregivers. This often affects your self-worth and self-esteem and leaves you feeling that you are to blame or that you had to be perfect to deserve love.

Feeling loved and accepted and having a sense of belonging is vital for human wellbeing. If this doesn't happen, we try to find ways to compensate or fixate on this particular need, potentially causing obsessive thoughts, depression, and BDD.

If you identify as LGBTQ+, you're even more likely to experience BDD, especially if you have experienced homophobia, biphobia, or transphobia. This kind of experience can also make you feel excluded and different from others, triggering a cascade of mental health challenges.

Low self-esteem

Self-esteem is the opinion we have of ourselves. If we have low self-esteem, it's more likely that we will view our lives through a negative lens, believe that we aren't good enough, and be less able to handle the challenges of life.

However, no baby is born with low self-esteem. It happens over the course of a lifetime as the result of our experiences and the messages we receive throughout our lives from parents, family members, siblings, friends, and other people we encounter, especially if one of these people was highly critical.

---

[8]   Causes of body dysmorphic disorder (BDD). Mind.org. (2022, July). Retrieved March 14, 2023, from https://www.mind.org.uk/information-support/types-of-mental-health-problems/body-dysmorphic-disorder-bdd/causes/

[9]   Amen, D. (2017, September 1). Can ostracism cause lingering pain in your brain? Amen Clinics Can Ostracism Cause Lingering Pain in Your Brain Comments. Retrieved March 13, 2023, from https://www.amenclinics.com/blog/ostracism-causes-lingering-pain-in-the-brain-2/

This can make you feel that you need to be 'perfect' if you want to live up to your own or others' expectations and deserve love.

Racism and BDD

Racism can also cause you to hold negative views about yourself because of society and how you've been treated because of the color of your skin. Note that even colorism – when someone treats you differently based on how dark or light your skin is – can trigger these feelings.

This, combined with the media's bias towards a certain look, can leave you feeling unaccepted by society, rejected, or that there is something intrinsically 'wrong' about your appearance. Your human desire to feel accepted means that you often believe you need to change something to be accepted or loved, and this can lead to obsessive thoughts about your appearance.

Fear of being rejected

Many BDD sufferers are faced with a fear of being rejected. Often, this is caused by poor attachment during childhood to a caregiver, perhaps believing that you needed to look or behave a certain way to be loved or accepted. If you suffered from abuse or trauma as a child, you are more likely to suffer from a Fearful-Avoidant attachment style which only adds fuel to the mental health fire. Bullying and other types of trauma can also have the same effect.

If you believe that the BDD symptoms you are experiencing are rooted in childhood trauma of any kind, seek the help of a therapist. I invite you to read my book *Healing Your Inner Child: 7 Beginner Steps to Reparent and Free Yourself From Childhood Trauma, Heal Deep Wounds and Live Life Authentically* , if you'd like to know more about the subject of inner child healing.

Perfectionism or comparing yourself with others

Often BDD is triggered or worsened when we compare ourselves to others, or we have perfectionist tendencies.

Since the advent of social media and the widespread use of airbrushing and filters, the problem has become even worse. We can't help comparing ourselves to these online images and believe that if we don't meet these unrealistic standards of beauty, we are flawed as human beings. This can be exacerbated if you are in fitness, bodybuilding, or modeling.

Genetics

There's also some evidence[10] that there is a genetic component to BDD—if you have a family history of depression, anxiety, OCD, or other mental health problems, you're more likely to suffer from BDD. Even if this only influences our sensitivity and reactions to negative experiences, it can have an effect on how we feel about our bodies and whether we suffer from obsessive thoughts.

Depression, anxiety, or OCD

As above, if you also have other mental health conditions, you are more likely to have BDD.

Is it really BDD?

Another issue with the BDD statistics is that many cases are misdiagnosed as other related conditions can be confused with BDD. What makes matters worse is that these related conditions can co-exist with BDD, making it challenging to separate them and reach an accurate diagnosis.

Perhaps this has happened to you. You've been diagnosed with depression, social anxiety disorder, or an eating disorder but feel that this isn't getting to the root of the problem, and so you continue to suffer with your symptoms.

If so, read through the list below that describes other mental health disorders and see whether you can relate.

Depression

Depression is a serious mood disorder that leads to a persistent feeling of sadness and a loss of interest in life and the things you used to enjoy. It can affect the way you think, feel, and behave and interfere with normal activities. If you suffer from depression, you can also believe that your life isn't worth living. BDD often causes symptoms of depression, amounting to a further problem that is hard to separate from the disorder itself.

---

[10]   What causes BDD? BDDF. (n.d.). Retrieved March 14, 2023, from https://bddfoundation.org/information/frequently-asked-questions/what-causes-bdd/

Social Anxiety Disorder

Social anxiety disorder, also called social phobia, is a long-term and overwhelming fear of social situations. Like BDD, it often starts during the teenage years and, like BDD, is also characterized by fears of being judged negatively by others.

Obsessive Compulsive Disorder (OCD)

Obsessive compulsive disorder is a mental health problem characterized by obsessive thoughts and compulsive behaviors. This usually starts around puberty and can worsen over the years as the sufferer attempts to maintain control of their life. In BDD, there may be a preoccupation with order and symmetry in appearance, which is very similar to OCD.

Eating Disorders

Eating disorders such as anorexia, bulimia, and binge eating disorder are mental health conditions where the sufferer uses food to cope with their feelings. This often starts during the teenage years and the sufferer may eat too much or too little or become obsessed with their weight or body shape.

Skin Picking Disorder / Dermatillomania

Skin picking disorder, or dermatillomania, is a mental illness related to OCD. The sufferer can't stop picking at their skin with their fingers, fingernails, teeth, or tools like tweezers, pins, and scissors, resulting in skin lesions and significant distress. Skin picking often occurs as a result of BDD.

Olfactory Reference Disorder

With olfactory reference disorder, the sufferer has an erroneous belief that they have a foul or unpleasant body odor. This can cause significant distress and result in repetitive behaviors like frequent showering, behavioral changes such as avoiding social situations, and even controlling their diet.

Body Integrity Identity Disorder

Body integrity identity disorder (BIID) is a rare mental health condition where the sufferer believes that there is a mismatch between their mental body image and their physical body. As a result, sufferers often wish to have a physical disability and want to amputate one or more healthy limbs or even become blind or deaf. Like BDD, it usually develops during the prepubescent years.

Borderline Personality Disorder

Borderline personality disorder (BDP) is a mental illness that impacts the sufferer's ability to regulate their emotions. This can lead to impulsivity and affect how the person feels about themselves, causing changes to their behavior and having a negative impact on relationships. Symptoms of BDD are very common for those with BPD.

Taijin Kyofu-Sho

Taijin kyofu-sho is a type of social anxiety found in Japan and parts of Asia. It's characterized by an intense fear that the body displeases, embarrasses, or offends others and is largely cultural in origin.

As you can see, there's a significant overlap between the disorders listed above and BDD.

Understanding yourself

By reading this far, you should have a good insight into the complexity of BDD, the symptoms you may suffer from and what could have caused or triggered the disorder to rear its ugly head.

However, this is just the tip of the iceberg. It doesn't help you define what is causing BDD to help you kickstart your healing process.

Before you can go any further, you must take time to reflect on your own experience of BDD and become more aware of your body image problems. After all, if you're sick and keep throwing up, you could just grab a bucket and struggle to cope with the symptoms as best you can. But if you really want to get better, it's a good idea to visit a doctor to check whether you have a stomach bug or other problem that could be treated.

Same goes for BDD. If you want to break free from this mental prison and get your life back, you must be brave and take time for some self-reflection, no matter how difficult or emotional this may be.

Please bear in mind that you must seek help if you're unsure of what you have so that you can ensure you're tackling the right condition.

Self-Reflection Exercises

To help you delve more deeply into your experience of BDD and find a path through, I'll be sharing some self-reflection exercises that you should find the time and space to complete. These go into more depth than the quiz we worked through in the last chapter and can help you to get clear on what you're facing.

Don't feel like you have to rush this process. Taking your time and being completely honest with yourself will make it more likely that you will heal and put this difficult period behind you.

So, grab a notebook and a pen, or find your phone and get ready to take some notes as we work through each in turn.

1. What is your problem feature?

- What do you dislike or want to improve?

- How concerned are you with each of these features? (Rate them on a scale of 1 to 10)

2. How noticeable is your feature to others?

It's not always easy to have insight into what others think. So, ask a trusted friend or therapist to rate your features from 1 to 10, but don't tell them how you rated them. Write down their answer or record another voice note.

3. Identify the severity of your body image symptoms

- How much time on an average day are you worried about your feature(s)?

- How often do you check or compare yourself with others?

- How much distress have these worries caused you?

- How much distress do you experience when confronted with a situation you wanted to avoid (such as a social situation)?

- How much do your worries interfere with your personal or professional life?

- How often have you avoided situations or activities because of your worries?

4. Identify your rituals and safety behaviors

What are you doing excessively because of your preoccupation? The following checklist might help…

- Checking your appearance in mirrors or other reflective surfaces.

- Checking your features by taking selfies.

- Checking your features by feeling them with your fingers.

- Using a particular light to check your features in a mirror.

- Wearing something to cover up your features or divert attention.

- Comparing your features with those you see in the media.

- Comparing your features to those you meet in person.

- Asking someone to confirm that your perceived defect exists.

- Seeking reassurance about your perceived defect.

5. Identify the impact of your symptoms on your life

How much do your symptoms affect your everyday life? (Rate them all on a scale of 1 to 10)

- If you're single, how much do your symptoms affect your dating life?

- If you are in a relationship, how do your symptoms affect it?

- How much do your symptoms affect your work or study life?

- How much do your symptoms affect your social life?

- How much do your symptoms affect your leisure activities?

- How do your symptoms interfere with your mental health?

- How much do they affect your everyday life?

Summary

Congratulations! By reading to the end of this chapter, you should now understand yourself much better and know that your experience of BDD isn't your fault! I commend you on taking this step and coming this far.

Many of us BDD sufferers feel like this because we already feel we are somehow 'abnormal', 'flawed' or 'broken' so shifting your perspective can help you find your own path through to healing.

We also worked through some self-reflection exercises that, hopefully you have already completed. If not, go ahead and do them now. By being brave, taking action and admitting that you are suffering from BDD, you can begin to transform your life.

Chapter 3

Setting Yourself Up for Success

"Those who cannot change their minds cannot change anything."

— George Bernard Shaw

Right now, you are standing at the cusp of a beautiful, happy, and fulfilling future.

You're standing at the peak of a mountain where you can look around you with a whole new perspective on life. You understand what could have led to your experience of BDD and that by choosing to take a different path, you can free yourself from its clutches.

You have the power over those obsessive and controlling thoughts – that negative inner voice that torments your existence – and you can choose to change. All you need to do is make the decision and then put the right steps into place and you can heal.

This chapter is the start of that change. As you read through, you will learn how to shift your thoughts so they become positive and empowering and therefore set the foundations in place for a brighter future. We'll be looking at that negative inner voice and how you can start to control it, how to create the right environment for positivity and healing, and how you can start on the right path right here and now.

Taking control of that negative inner voice

As I mentioned just a moment ago, the core problem with BDD is that negative voice in your head that tells you that you aren't good enough, criticizes your appearance and actions, points out your flaws, and attacks you for not meeting its high standards.

Even those who don't have BDD often struggle with this negative inner voice and, rather than master it, try to find ways they can 'deal' with its presence.

But for us BDD sufferers, this negative voice becomes unbearable, accelerating and gaining power over us until we are left cowering in a corner or believe that what it says is true.

Usually, this voice is simply reflecting the thoughts and words of people who criticized you in the past. You might even have flashbacks to those events or even 'hear' the words in the voice of your psychological attacker.

And more often than not, we believe what it tells us. We confuse it with our conscience and use it to guide our behavior, worsening our mental health and feeding the BDD symptoms.

But we have got it completely wrong. Whilst this voice is indeed a mechanism designed to protect us from harm, it has the opposite effect. Even if we manage to ignore it, it ends up attacking us from the inside when we least expect it. It becomes like a festering wound that we try to hide with a band-aid. But without the attention and treatment it needs, it ends up so infected that we're in pain and we can ignore it no more.

When I was deep in my period of self-reflection, I realized that the only way I could heal was to make friends with this inner voice, acknowledge it was there, listen to what it had to share but then take control, thank it for its input but then understand that it was wrong.

Many people find it useful to give a name to this voice. Perhaps you know of a character in a movie or TV show that's always negative, you could name your inner critic after them or give yours any nickname you want. By doing this, you can distance yourself from it, reduce its power over your life and start to break the obsessive cycle of negative thoughts that are responsible for BDD.

Now I want you to find a name for your negative inner voice and write it down somewhere you can see it often. You'll need this in your journey.

Developing the right mindset

Once you've started to control your negative inner voice, you'll also need to set the foundations for better mental health and recovery.

Adopting the right mindset can be the single most powerful factor when you do this. It can make the difference between you trying (and struggling) to recover and actually succeeding.

So, what is mindset? According to the Berkley Wellbeing Institute, "Mindset is defined as the set of attitudes or beliefs that we hold."[11]

Our mindset is the lens through which we perceive the world; it influences our thoughts, feelings, behaviors and how we respond to different situations and influences. It shapes our experience as people and also influences our motivation, self-belief and what we achieve in our lives.

Interestingly, we aren't born with a predefined mindset. Instead, it develops over time as we are exposed to the thoughts, opinions, and behaviors of our caregivers, family, friends, and those we come into contact with, our culture, social norms, learning environment, and our experiences.

Our mindset works as a type of blueprint for our lives. It helps us make sense of what we are experiencing, set our expectations and help keep us safe.

It's very common to hold onto mindsets that helped us at one point but now keep us trapped or limit our lives. For example, if you were betrayed at a young age, you might have difficulty trusting people because of what you experienced. However, if you continue to view others with suspicion and a lack of trust, you could have difficulty forming relationships.

Likewise, if someone pointed out a certain body feature when you were younger and mocked, teased, humiliated, or made fun of you because of it, you are likely to be more self-conscious about that feature and attempt to hide it or resort to those obsessive mirrors checking behaviors that we see with BDD.

Although there are many different types of mindsets, we can broadly split them into two groups—a fixed mindset and a growth mindset.

---

[11] Mindsets: Definition, examples, and books (growth, fixed + other types). The Berkeley Well-Being Institute. (n.d.). Retrieved March 14, 2023, from https://www.berkeleywellbeing.com/mindsets.html

What is a fixed mindset?

A fixed mindset is when you believe that your personal qualities are set in stone and cannot be changed. You believe that you are either 'good' or 'bad' at something such as playing football or learning a foreign language, that failures are a reflection of your innate abilities and that it's not worth trying new experiences, learning new things or working on yourself because it just won't work.

It's common for us sufferers of BDD to get trapped in this mindset, believing that we can never move through these difficult times because it's just who we are. We believe that trying to escape its clutches would be a waste of time and effort and we'd be better off just surviving the best we can.

Often a fixed mindset means that people are constantly using their performance to try to confirm their intelligence, personality and character, prove their worth or seek validation. Do you see the similarities here with BDD?

What is a growth mindset?

A growth mindset is when you believe that your qualities can change depending on how much time, effort, and persistence you invest. With a growth mindset, there's no such thing as being 'bad' or 'good' at anything and any challenge is an opportunity to reflect, learn and grow.

You are better able to persist through obstacles, learn from criticism and find inspiration from others' successes so you can build the life (and mental health) that you dream of.

I expect you can see where I'm going here. If you can develop a growth mindset, you will understand that you aren't trapped in this traumatic, stressful, and difficult place. Perhaps more importantly, you'll understand that BDD doesn't define you.

Let me say that again because it is key to your recovery.

BDD doesn't define you. You aren't a person who HAS the disorder but someone who is currently experiencing it.

You can change. You can take control of those obsessive thoughts, gain relief from that incessant and toxic negative voice inside your head, throw off those chains and get your life back. You can gain strength and inspiration from the fact that I'm here talking to you today as a person who has experienced exactly what you have and I've healed. You can do the same.

Which do you have? Fixed or growth mindset?

First, let's explore which of these two types of mindsets you have so you can start to shift into a healthier way of seeing yourself and the world.

Grab your pen and paper, open up that document on your laptop or fire up your voice recorder app and work through the following questions, noting down which of the statements you agree with:

- You're born with a certain amount of intelligence and you can't change it.

- There isn't much you can do to improve your personality or abilities.

- People either have particular talents, or they don't. You can't just acquire talent for things like music, writing, art, or athletics.

- People can change who they are and how they think

- You can learn new things and improve your intelligence.

- Studying, working hard, and practicing new skills are all ways to develop new talents and abilities.

Which of these statements did you agree with? If you said yes to questions 1 to 3, you are likely to have a fixed mindset. On the other hand, if you answered yes to questions 4 to 6, you are likely to have a growth mindset.

You can change your mindset

The good news is that you can change your mindset, shift your thoughts to positive ones and liberate yourself from BDD. Best of all, you'll also be setting yourself up for a bright and promising future, even when BDD is only a distant memory.

Of course, I'm not claiming that switching your mindset is a cure for BDD. Nor that it's some kind of shortcut to better mental health. But it will help you regain control over your life, embrace challenges and opportunities that come your way and help you to grow as a person and live a rich and fulfilling life.

We can change our mindsets because the brain is neuroplastic. This means that all those connections within your brain can continue to grow, change, and reorganize throughout your life, no matter how old you are or what you have been through.

You have the power to feel better.

Changing your mindset can raise your happiness

The Dalai Lama proclaims that there are two ways to reach contentment. Either acquire everything you want and desire or feel grateful for what you already possess.

In the case of those with BDD, we can chase contentment by working out, eating, or undergoing surgery until we have the 'perfect body', but this is a black hole that leads to disaster and despair. Why? Well, because we've already determined that for those with BDD, contentment will never come—there will always be something to 'fix' because our bodies aren't the problem; it's our minds.

If we can change our mindset to one of accepting and loving the body we have, we will feel so much happier with our existence. The mindset shift is from craving the 'perfect' look to accepting, being content with, and then learning to love the body we have. Gratitude for what you have will help you reach this place of contentment.

How can you cultivate a positive mindset?

As mentioned above, we can help ourselves break free from BDD if we can shift our mindsets and become more positive.

Back when I was in the grips of the disorder, I would have laughed in your face if you suggested that this was possible. I was so totally consumed by negative and obsessive thoughts about my body and life that escape seemed impossible.

Although there were times I wished that my life was different and that I was 'normal', usually I just felt hopeless and miserable. Why bother trying to heal when it's impossible, right?

In some ways, it would have been easier to stay on the same path and remain a victim. I wouldn't have to find the strength and push myself to find that light on the horizon, change my habits or even control the effect that the negative inner voice was having on me.

But I soon learned that I was stronger than I thought. I could train myself to see things in a new light, push away those clouds of suffering and doubt to see the promise of blue sky and start my healing journey.

In this section, I want to show you exactly how you can do this.

1. Accept yourself

Before anything else, we need to learn to accept where we are. We need to accept our struggles with BDD, acknowledge that we do have a problem, recognize the effect that our thoughts and behaviors have on our lives and tell ourselves that it's OK to feel like this.

In fact, that's exactly what we have been doing with the exercises in the previous chapters. If you skipped forward without doing those exercises, please go back and work your way through them. This part of the book will still be here when you're done.

Additionally, you need to know that it's OK if those thoughts do show up because you can cope with them and can continue on your healing path. By doing this, you are telling your brain that you don't care when the BDD symptoms show up and it slowly starts to lose its power over you.

It's also extremely empowering to know that you can deal with whatever arises. Even if you aren't 100% sure that you can cope, simply acting as if you do can help push those repetitive thoughts into the background and help you get on with your life. The power balance begins to shift when you do this—your thoughts are no longer in control of you. Rather, it's the other way around.

There are many tools and resources you can use to help you foster this attitude, the most powerful of which is mindfulness meditation. I'll be going into more detail about meditation in Chapter 6.

2. Identify Your Values

Any kind of body image issue tends to emerge or worsen when we become too focused on our appearance and continuously compare it to people around us and the images we see in the media.

When we are focused on our appearance, we tend to forget that we have so much more to offer the world. The first step to helping you break this preoccupation is to understand what really matters to you and what you want your life to stand for. When you can identify these, you can use them to guide the direction you want your life to take. You can start to control your thoughts, behaviors, and overall attitude to life and start moving towards a calmer and happier life.

Exercise: How to identify your values

To identify your values, find a quiet place and consider the following questions. Make sure you are completely honest with yourself and don't rush the process.

1. What parts of life would you be engaging in or enjoying if you weren't preoccupied with your appearance? What activities would you take part in? What interests would you like to pursue?

2. What would you do if you weren't afraid of what other people think or if you weren't afraid of failing?

3. What did you use to love or value before you developed BDD or body image issues?

4. Which of the following values are most important to you? Pick five from this list.[12]

- Authenticity

- Achievement

- Adventure

- Authority

- Autonomy

- Balance

- Beauty

- Boldness

- Compassion

- Challenge

- Citizenship

- Community

- Competency

- Contribution

- Creativity

- Curiosity

---

[12]   The LEADERSHAPE Institute. Boise State University. (2022, May). Retrieved March 14, 2023, from https://www.boisestate.edu/getinvolved/lead/leadershape/

- Meaningful Work
- Openness
- Optimism
- Peace
- Pleasure
- Poise
- Popularity
- Recognition
- Religion
- Reputation
- Respect
- Responsibility
- Security
- Self-Respect
- Service
- Spirituality
- Stability
- Success
- Status

- Determination
- Fairness
- Faith
- Fame
- Friendships
- Fun
- Growth
- Happiness
- Honesty
- Humor
- Influence
- Inner Harmony
- Justice
- Kindness
- Knowledge
- Leadership
- Learning
- Love
- Loyalty

- Trustworthiness

- Wealth

- Wisdom

Once you've worked through the questions above and identified your five key values, you can use these to guide you through your healing journey. I identified mine, wrote them out on Post-it notes, and put them throughout my home so I could see them often. You might like to do the same. Then ask yourself, how can you experience more of these values in your life?

3. Describe your goals

If you want to overcome your symptoms of BDD and regain control of your life, it isn't enough to simply wish that your life was better. You need to know exactly what you would change to get to this place—in other words, set some goals for yourself.

Although these goals can be anything you want them to be, it's better to start by reviewing your perceived 'problem features' and your coping behaviors so you can gradually regain control step by step.

1. Start by reviewing the answers you gave in the last chapter regarding these perceived 'problem' features and your coping behaviors.

2. Next, think about how you could slightly challenge your current behaviors so you could gain control and use these to create either one or several short-term goals. For example, if you believe that your skin is a problem feature, you might set the following goals: Stop comparing your skin to others, limit how frequently you engage in skin-picking behaviors, make a conscious effort to try not be overly critical, and, if the BDD symptoms have kept you from socializing, make a coffee date with a trusted friend.

3. Then think about some medium-term goals that will challenge you more but aren't too overwhelming. Remember that these are goals that will take longer to achieve so you don't have to feel overwhelmed at this point by the whole idea. This could include meeting up with friends, leaving the house without makeup or even enjoying certain leisure activities again.

4. Finally, consider some long-term goals that will help you see the bigger picture, give you something to aim towards and, again, remind you that

there is light at the end of the tunnel! This could be starting to date again, learning a new skill or language or finding a new career. Long term goals can be anywhere between one year to several—it's up to you to decide!

Make sure that you don't include anything physical in your goals such as using new products, visiting a cosmetic surgeon or signing up for the gym. These will only add fuel to the BDD fire and make it even harder to recover.

Once you've established your goals, decide on your action plan. What are the first baby steps you could take to reach your short-term goals? The size of the steps don't matter. What matters is that you're heading in the right direction! Just go with it!

4. Find positive friends

We are the average of the five people we spend the most time with, according to motivational speaker, Jim Rohn.[13] This means that if you're surrounded by negative or highly critical people, you will also feel more negative and critical of yourself and the world around you.

If you can find a positive social circle, you can start to shift your mindset, control those negative thoughts and feel empowered to make the change you so desperately need in your life.

For me, this meant letting go of those friendships that drained my energy and pulled me down. Some of my friends spent so much time complaining about their lives and their appearance and gossiping about other people that it was a toxic environment for me to be in and one that I needed to change.

However, I am certainly not telling you to ditch your friends, especially if they are also going through a tough time or suffer from BDD as you do. But what I do suggest is that you review your friendships and consider whether the friendship is helping or harming you. At times, this could simply mean setting boundaries such as asking them not to talk about appearance when you are with them so that you aren't triggered.

I would also encourage you to find a tribe that reflects the values that you want to adopt. Search online for these groups or if you can, consider joining meetups and social events to help you get to know these people better.

---

13   Rohn, J. (n.d.). You're the average of the five people you spend the most time with. Business Insider. Retrieved March 14, 2023, from https://www.businessinsider.com/jim-rohn-youre-the-average-of-the-five-people-you-spend-the-most-time-with-2012-7

Over time, it will become easier to connect with these positive people who lift you up instead of drag you down.

5. Review your social media consumption

It's no secret that social media can trigger or worsen a lot of body image and mental health issues because we can't help but compare ourselves to the flawless images we see.

Luckily, we know that much of what we see online is airbrushed, photoshopped, filtered, and tweaked until the person is far from what they actually look like in real life. What's worse is that social media often portrays only what people want you to see and NOT what they are actually like. And yet we still compare ourselves harshly and struggle when our lives and appearances don't meet these unrealistic ideals. For that reason, I'd highly encourage you to avoid or restrict your use of social media until you have healed.

You could start by unfriending or unfollowing people that make you feel worse, such as those with altered photos or flashy lifestyles and body images. Instead, follow inspirational or motivational accounts that can keep you happy and help you in your journey.

Another option is to pause or delete your social media accounts altogether. This is exactly what I did, although I did make sure I had the phone numbers of everyone I wanted to stay in contact with and told them that I wouldn't be using those sites for a while.

Of course, it wasn't exactly easy to break that habit in the beginning, but I'm so glad that I did. My life has completely transformed for the better since I took this step.

6. Avoid all "bad news"

It's not only those unrealistic, hyper-altered images on social media that can affect our mental health. It's also the news. When we see constant stories of war, murder, politics, corruption, climate change, economic crises, poverty, famine, and natural disasters, we can't help but feel affected. We are human beings and we care, even if these events are happening thousands of miles away.

What's more, we are bringing more negative energy into our brains and wasting our thoughts on something that we simply cannot change.

That's why we should also consider how often we watch the news and what news we are consuming. If you watch every news bulletin throughout the day, you will be overwhelmed with negativity, so try cutting back to just once per day. It's also a good idea to look for sources of positive media that emphasize and remind us of the good in life and help us develop a more positive mindset.

7. *Listen to more music*

Did you know that when we listen to music, our bodies release the 'reward hormone' known as dopamine which leaves us feeling great? It can also help ease depression, lower our stress levels, boost our mood, and even help improve our brain power. Lyrics affect our thoughts, especially if we are singing along at the same time. With that in mind, I'd encourage you to listen to more music… BUT be careful what you are listening to. Only choose music that leaves you feeling calm, uplifted, energized, and positive with inspiring, feel-good, and motivational lyrics, not the kind that talk about looks, bodies, or any form of negativity.

Why not spend some time looking for uplifting songs and create a playlist you can listen to whenever you want musical therapy?

8. *Choose positive shows and movies*

Everything around us has an influence on how we see the world. All that information we are consuming gets subconsciously stored in our brains and can be retrieved later, even if we aren't aware of it. So, if we're watching a lot of what makes us feel insecure such as unrealistic bodies and lifestyles, or topics that bring stress to our lives, it's no wonder we can get trapped in a cycle of obsessive thought and negativity.

Instead, try watching more meaningful shows where the people have realistic bodies and lifestyles and that carry a positive message. These can include uplifting documentaries, motivational reality shows, inspiring talks, nature shows, comedies, and so on. There's so much content available from many streamlining platforms that it's often easy to find something you love and avoid the things that trigger BDD symptoms.

I have a challenge for you. I want you to go and look for three positive shows today. Write them down, and then give them a try this week. I'm sure you'll notice the difference.

9. *Mirror Checking*

OK, it's time to tackle a tricky one—checking yourself in the mirror.

Around 90% of BDD sufferers check themselves in a mirror or other reflective surfaces multiple times per day, either to ease their fears about how they look or to confirm that their perceived flaw is still present and still as bad as before.

Although this may seem harmless, it can turn into an obsession as the person examines their perceived flaws in close detail, feeds their anxiety, and adds up to multiple hours per day.

Yes, mirrors are useful, but only if they're used in moderation and for the right reasons. If we allow ourselves to be consumed by checking our appearance and continue with this mirror-checking ritual, we are feeding the obsessive thought beast.

That's why you should also limit the time you check yourself in the mirror, and if you can, avoid mirrors as much as possible. Here are some tips:

1. Review

Start by considering how many times you check your appearance in the mirror and for how long each time, then aim to reduce this. I found that by resisting my urges and cutting my time in half, I was able to break the cycle and start to regain control.

2. Develop coping skills

It's a good idea to develop a toolkit of activities or coping skills you can turn to as a replacement for your mirror checking. I find that spending more time preparing my food, going for a walk, journaling, or even meditating can help me through.

3. Cover up your bathroom mirrors

This one seems harsh, but it can really help to break the ritual and make any mirror checking more intentional and purposeful. When your mirrors are covered, in order to look in them you need to remove the cover. This will give you the time to think twice—do I really need to look in the mirror now? Why not find a funky fabric that you love to make the experience fun? Mine is a purple velvet mini curtain that I fixed right over the mirror to add some theatrical drama! What could you add?

4. Use affirmations

When you do use your mirror for legitimate reasons, it's a good idea to use affirmations. Don't let the word put you off—this simply means saying positive statements while you look at yourself to plant seeds of positivity in your thoughts so that, over time, you eventually believe them. If you'd like to know more about Mirror Work, I recommend the book 'Heal Your Body' by Louise Hay.[14]

[14]   https://www.amazon.com/Heal-Your-Body-Louise-Hay/dp/0937611352

10. *Create a positive mindset morning routine*

I always found that my thoughts were at their darkest in the morning when I was still feeling groggy from sleep. Those negative thoughts about my body and life would always creep through and then it felt like there was little I could do to shake it off. I knew that if I wanted to tackle my symptoms and create a positive environment for my day, something needed to change.

That's why I decided to create a morning routine that would help clear my mind, focus on the positive and improve my overall health. I'd highly encourage you to do the same. What you decide to do really depends on you, but I suggest doing one or several of the following:

- Practice a 10-minute meditation or visualization.

- Listen to personal growth videos, audiobooks, or podcasts.

- Do a short workout (to get those feel-good endorphins flowing).

- Stretch or practice yoga.

- Make a mental list of the things you're looking forward to that day.

- Start a gratitude practice: name ten things you are grateful for.

How to get the help and support you need

As much as we often want to believe, we can't cope with the pressures and struggles of life alone because it's who we are as human beings.

We all need to know that there is a community around us that can provide us with the understanding, support and guidance we need when things get tough. That's why, as well as seeking professional help from a therapist, you should also consider growing a support network.

This can include anyone from friends, family members and partners to support groups, accountability partners and even specialized professionals such as nutritional therapists, yoga or meditation teachers and so on.

Support groups

When you join a support group, you'll know that the people around you understand exactly what you are going through, accept you exactly as you are, share their own stories and even provide useful tips or resources that can help you get better. They also provide a place you can speak openly and honestly without fear of judgment and you can possibly make friends along the way.

The BDD Foundation has compiled a fantastic list of online support groups that you can attend from your own home, so go through the list and see if there's anything that will fit. Otherwise, you can hit Google and search for BDD support group [insert your location] to find both online and face-to-face meetups.

Facebook can also be an excellent source of support groups so it's well worth checking out too. I created a BDD Facebook group myself, and I invite you to join the community. Please add me on Facebook to find out more.

Accountability partners

Over the years I suffered from BDD, there were so many times that I vowed that I'd find a way to heal so I could ease that mental torture, break those obsessive thoughts and habits and regain my life. But time after time, I'd give up after just a few days, thinking that it was just too hard, or too painful, or that, even if I did focus on healing, it wouldn't work anyway because BDD was part of who I was. Or so I believed.

It was only when I found an accountability partner that I broke free and finally found my path to healing.

An accountability partner is simply someone who can be there to support you and help you reach your goals. They could be on the same path as you, or they could be someone close to you, such as a friend or family member. It really doesn't matter. The fact that you have someone else who is invested in your wellbeing can help you stick to this positive path and break free from BDD.

I found my accountability partner via the BDD support group that I was attending at the time. How could you find yours?

Nutritionists

A huge part of your body image issues and mental health can be tied to your lifestyle habits, especially what you eat.

If you're not giving your body what it needs to thrive, your mental health can take a blow, and any anxiety, trauma or stress you are dealing with can feel even more intense and unmanageable. This is especially the case if you also have an eating disorder or your eating habits fluctuate between extremes as a result of your stress levels or BDD symptoms.

It may be a good idea to make an appointment with a nutritionist who can check what you are eating and provide suggestions on how you can eat better and stay healthy. Because they are qualified medical professionals, they won't give you advice that could trigger an eating disorder but rather, help you to stay on track and provide your body with what it needs, address body image and weight concerns, and even explore hunger and fullness cues.

Summary

Wow you've received a lot of information in this chapter, haven't you? You've learned how to shift your mindset, tackle that negative inner voice, cultivate a positive mindset, identify your values and feel more positive and empowered with a variety of easy tools you can use every day to feel better. Make sure you work through the exercises I've included so that you can really set yourself up for success moving forward. In the wise words of Dr. Seuss, *"Only you can control your future"*.

Chapter 4

Regain Control

"Motivation is what gets you started. Habit is what keeps you going."

— Jim Rohn

Perhaps the biggest issue with BDD is that it steals any control you may feel you have over your life.

You become a victim of the whims of that negative inner voice and are unable to believe in your own value as a human, stand up for what you believe in, and enjoy healthy relationships with those around you. How could you, when you feel so tormented by what is happening in your head?

However, you can break free from this prison and start to reclaim control, feel empowered to live a positive life and start to open up about how you are feeling – especially to those who love and care for you.

The first steps in this process are learning to set healthy boundaries, monitoring your habits and getting them under control, and then fostering open communication with your friends and loved ones so they can understand and support you and your healing journey.

In this chapter, I'll walk you through this part of the process, showing you that you have the power within to push further toward healing and discover a happier and healthier life.

The relationship between personal boundaries and BDD

As we know, when we are suffering from BDD, we have a somewhat difficult relationship with ourselves and the world around us.

Our obsessive thought patterns mean that we tend to view life through a different lens, believing that we are being judged or criticized by others and that because of our 'flaw', we have less value as human beings.

Not only do we believe that our voices, opinions, dreams, and desires don't matter, but we can also end up developing a love-hate relationship with other people. While we feel lonely and crave human interaction and approval, we can often reject it.

We're afraid of letting people get too close because we fear their disapproval or judgment or believe that they will somehow let us down or place high demands on us that we simply can't reach.

This is exactly what happened to me every time I got into a relationship. Insecurity, obsessive thoughts, and a desire to please the special person in my life meant that I was often unbearable to be around. In other cases, they put so much pressure on my shoulders that I ended up feeling resentful, disappointed, and overwhelmed.

Take my ex-fiancée, for example. Our relationship was beautiful when it first started. Although I was still battling those obsessive thoughts about my appearance, I was so focused on expressing my desire and showering my special person with affection that we fell head over heels in love.

But it was only a matter of time before the cracks started to show. I constantly needed reassurance about my appearance and felt insanely jealous and insecure if someone else just glanced at my partner. Our love slowly dissolved into arguments and conflict.

What's worse is that it ended up feeling like some kind of child-parent relationship where my partner would make all the decisions, provide the emotional support I needed, and take control of our lives. Yes, this was comforting and supportive. But in the end, I felt like a victim of my obsessive thoughts and my partner's whims and desires. I'd lost my sense of empowerment and control and was often taken advantage of because I felt like I had to give back when my partner had given so much.

When my partner lashed out at me, accusing me of being vain and self-obsessed before walking out of my life, I knew I had to change. This wasn't only the start of my journey to healing from BDD but also the time when I realized I had to do something about my personal boundaries.

What are personal boundaries?

Personal boundaries are simply an invisible line that defines what we're willing to accept and what we're not.

There are many different types of boundaries, including:

- Physical
How we feel about physical affection such as hugs and kisses as well as ideas of personal space, privacy, and our body.

- Sexual
What is acceptable to us in our sex lives.

- Intellectual
This concerns our thoughts and beliefs and whether someone accepts or dismisses your ideas and opinions.

- Emotional
Whether you share your feelings with friends, a partner, and those around you.

- Time
How much time you're willing to give to others.

Many people have strict boundaries and are very aware of what they want, what they believe, what they're willing to accept, and how closely they guard their needs. They keep people distant and can often seem detached and emotionless, have few friendships, and may avoid other people.

Others, especially BDD sufferers, lack these boundaries for the reasons that I've mentioned above. They get overly involved with other people's problems, find it difficult to say no, and find themselves catering to the whims of other people, even if it has a negative impact on their physical, emotional, or psychological health, because they fear rejection.

Our personal boundaries are usually based on our upbringing, culture, and experiences and can shift over the course of our lives.

Why are boundaries important?

Having healthy personal boundaries is vital if we want to live a rich, fulfilling, happy, and balanced life.

If we lack boundaries or they're too extreme, we can suffer enormously, lacking the ability to live according to our own values (see Chapter 3), feeling isolated and lonely, hurt by others, and suffering from self-esteem issues. We can end up being taken advantage of by people who don't respect us or that don't realize that we have our limits too.

By learning to clearly define our boundaries, we can take control of our lives, free ourselves even more from BDD, and start to live life on our own terms.

We can also:

- Make our expectations clear to others.

- Develop our sense of self-respect.

- Understand our needs and honor them.

- Communicate our needs effectively.

- Stay safe.

- Reduce our stress levels and promote better health.

- Boost our self-esteem.

- Stop needing approval from others.

- Overcome learned helplessness and fear of being rejected or criticized.

As I spent more time reflecting on my personal boundaries, I understood that I was a true people pleaser and did things that other people wanted me to because I wanted to be accepted.

I constantly pushed my limits and felt like the world always wanted something from me, pushing my own needs into the background, believing that people would think I was bad or selfish if I said no. This only led to me feeling overwhelmed, resentful, angry, and often traumatized by accepting situations that I really shouldn't have.

Quiz: Do you have healthy boundaries?

Before we look at ways we can start setting healthier boundaries and put our own needs first, I'd like us to review our existing boundaries. Review the following statements and see which resonates with you the most.

1. Do you…

    a) Protect yourself from being taken advantage of?

    b) Find that other people often use you or take advantage of you?

2. Do you…

    a) Protect your time?

    b) Overcommit your time and leave little to yourself?

3. Do you…

    a) Have healthy self-respect and self-esteem?

    b) Suffer from a critical inner voice and have low self-esteem?

4. Do you…

    a) Only take on responsibilities you can handle?

    b) Feel exhausted or burnt out by overwhelming responsibilities and commitments?

5. Can you…

    a) Say 'no' if you don't want to do something?

    b) Find it difficult to say 'no'?

6. Do you…

   a) Set limits for others without feeling bad?

   b) Feel guilty for expressing boundaries?

7. Do you…

   a) Have a strong sense of identity and direction?

   b) Change yourself to fit in with different people?

8. Do you…

   a) Take care of your own problems and understand that you cannot heal other people's issues for them?

   b) Take on other people's problems as your own?

9. Do you…

   a) Clearly communicate your needs and wants and prioritize self-care?

   b) Put other people's needs and wants before your own?

Once you've looked at the questions, add up how many times you answered (b). If you agree with one or more of the statements, you need to work on setting healthier boundaries so you can protect your health and live your most authentic life.

How to start setting healthy boundaries

Personal boundaries are a very individual thing; what is acceptable or even good to one person might not be to the other. That's why we need to first take time to self-reflect before getting clear on our boundaries, communicating them with others, and reclaiming our personal power.

Here are the steps I want you to take.

1. Take time for self-reflection

Find some time to sit in a quiet space with a notebook and consider what you are willing to accept or not accept. I understand that this can feel overwhelming, so I've provided a few prompts below to get you started. Work through the questions, then make note of your answers.

- How do you feel about your interactions with others? Do they bring you pleasure and comfort or stress?

- Why do you think you feel like this after interacting with them?

- What would you change about these interactions?

- What makes you feel safe, supported, and understood?

- What were the key values that you identified in Chapter 3? Write them down again.

- Do you feel that you are living according to these values?

- How could you start aligning your life with these values?

- What do you think is causing your stress or discomfort in your interactions with others?

- Are there any people around you that cause stress or leave you feeling drained? Who are they? Why do you think you end up feeling like this?

- If you could change anything about the way people treat you, what would it be?

2. *Write down your boundaries*

After you've worked through the above questions, we're going to get creative and start to outline what your boundaries are.

To start, grab a large piece of paper; the bigger, the better. Then draw a large circle in the middle of the paper. This circle represents what you accept and the space outside this circle is what you're not willing to accept.

Write your reflections from the last step here, placing what you're not willing to accept outside of the circle and what you accept inside. Use different colored pens if you can to help make this display of your boundaries more visual and exciting.

That's it. You should be clear now on the basic framework of your boundaries. However, this isn't where your journey will stop. Continue to spend time thinking about your boundaries and add to this chart whenever you want to so you can keep growing your personal strength, self-esteem, confidence, and sense of self.

3. Start living according to these boundaries

Knowing what your boundaries are is only the first step towards living them. If you want to live a rich and fulfilling life, you also need to communicate your boundaries to others. This can be challenging, especially if we are people pleasers and worry about rejection. However, people aren't mind readers and won't know unless you tell them.

Most people will respect your boundaries, respect you for sharing them, and will apologize if they overstep the mark. If not, it's time to reconsider whether you really want them in your life.

For example, let's say that your best friend is constantly aware of people's appearance and will frequently make critical, judgmental, or other types of comments. For most BDD sufferers, this can feed the negative obsessive thought cycle, which is why you may have included it in your list of boundaries. If you want to express that this is unacceptable to you, you should carefully explain this to your friend. Start by pointing out their behavior, explain why you understand, explain why this is a problem for you, then tell them what you'd like them to do instead. Here's an example of what this might look like.

"I wanted to talk to you about something. I've noticed that you often mention other people's appearance and criticize what they are wearing. When you do this when I'm around, it can be very triggering and makes me even more aware of my current experience of BDD and mental health problems. It would really help my recovery if you could avoid doing this when I'm around."

Here are some more examples:

- "I don't have the energy to help you with [their request] right now, but maybe [this resource] can help."

- "I can only stay for an hour".

- "If you're going to be late, please let me know ahead of time."

- "I understand you're having a hard time, and I want to be there for you, but I don't have the emotional capacity to listen right now."

- "It makes me feel uncomfortable when you [touch or act]. If you can't respect my space, I'll have to leave."

- "This is not a topic I'm willing to discuss right now."

- "I don't find those types of comments funny."

- "I understand we see things differently, and I respect your opinion, but please don't force it on me."

- "Please ask me first before borrowing my [possession]" or "I would appreciate it if you didn't touch my [material thing]."

- "I don't feel comfortable with you posting that on Instagram."

4. Be consistent

Once you've set your personal boundaries, you need to consistently enforce them to avoid confusion, stress, tension, and upset or even falling back into those unhealthy patterns.

I understand that this can be hard, especially if you really want to help a friend or feel bad about letting people down. But this is how you reclaim and retain your personal power.

If you're struggling, think of it like toilet training a pet dog. You need to have these rules in place and stick to them each and every time if you want him or her to stop using your home as a bathroom. Just one moment of weakness can make it even harder to train them and can even take them back to step one. You don't want to jeopardize your growing sense of self with one moment of doubt or weakness. Stick to it!

How to learn the art of open communication

Once I'd reflected on my boundaries and defined them using the same exercise I mentioned above, I knew that I needed to share them with others if they were going to make a difference to my mental health and life.

But there was just one problem—I kept coming up against several mental blocks. No matter how much I wanted to heal, I couldn't get over the fear and vulnerability that the mere thought of sharing my feelings sparked in me.

I'll be honest, there was a point where I thought that all the work that I'd done up until this point felt futile. I found myself wondering whether it was really possible to heal from **BDD** because I simply couldn't take this vital step.

It was only when I read the following quote that I could shift my mindset and take that first step…

"We speak not only to tell other people what we think, but to tell ourselves what we think. Speech is a part of thought" – Oliver Sacks

Learning how to communicate openly with others and express my needs wasn't only about telling the world about my non-negotiables. It was also part of my healing journey itself. By opening up the conversation, I'd also be reminding myself of what was important to me and strengthening that sense of self-empowerment and confidence. This could be one of the final pieces of the puzzle—the step that would help me get even closer to a happy and fulfilling life.

Why is open communication important for your healing journey?

As I learned, open communication isn't only about sharing your boundaries with the world but can also help you reinforce your sense of personal power.

Additionally, it can be a powerful way to help your loved ones, friends, and people around you to understand exactly what you are going through and how you are working towards healing from BDD.

By sharing your feelings, they can become your support system, help you feel understood and less isolated and even help change your environment so you can stop any potential BDD triggers and heal faster.

At the same time, these people will feel less shut out and can make better sense of your behavior, strengthening the relationship and sense of trust at the same time.

It's not always easy, especially if you are the type of person who prefers to keep their problems to themselves.

For example, you may have grown up in a family or culture that didn't express their emotions or believe that sharing feelings or problems is a sign of weakness.

You might also worry about the other person's reactions, believing that they will be angry or reject you. This is made worse if you feel like you are the only person who has these issues or if you're deep in mental anguish and struggling to make sense of your own feelings.

How to start opening up

If you truly want to heal, develop stronger relationships, and feel supported, happy, and self-empowered, you need to learn to share your feelings instead of hiding them. Even if you believe that you're 'not the sharing type', this can help accelerate your recovery so you can break free from the clutches of BDD faster.

There are many online resources that can help you learn the art of open communication but I found them to be complex and overwhelming. Instead, I encourage you to follow the steps I'm about to share. It took time but they worked for me and I trust they will work for you too.

1. Why do you want to share your feelings?

Do you want to foster open communication so you can help your loved ones understand what you are going through? Speak about your boundaries? Get the support that you need? Think about this before you start any conversation.

2. Start small

You don't need to dive in headfirst and share your most intimate thoughts and feelings with those around you. In fact, this can have the opposite effect on your life and wellbeing. Instead, choose the people you trust the most, such as a friend, partner, sibling, or therapist.

3. Choose a suitable time and place and the right method of communication

When you're sharing for the first time, it's important to feel as comfortable as possible to make the process easier for everyone involved. Start by deciding whether you'd prefer a face-to-face conversation, text message, phone call, letter, or email. Then find a comfortable place where you're unlikely to be disturbed and set a time for the conversation to happen. This will keep you accountable and encourage you to follow through with your decision.

4. Practice makes perfect

Before you have the conversation, think about what you want to say in as much detail as you want. If it will help, make notes to help you express yourself more clearly and jog your memory during the conversation itself.

5. Tell them what you want them to do

At the end of the conversation, it's helpful to express what you'd like the other person to do. This could involve simply being there as a listening ear, providing emotional support, respecting your boundaries or providing practical help such as finding the right BDD resources, experts or therapists to help you on your healing journey.

6. Reflect on the experience

After you have this conversation, take time to think about how it felt. What felt comfortable? What felt uncomfortable? What would you do next time? What else might help? Make notes afterward so that you can refer back to them and make adjustments going forward. For example, if you chose to have the conversation in a restaurant but found the environment too distracting, opt for a quieter space, like a park.

Remember that having one conversation is just the start.

People need time to absorb and make sense of the information that you have shared, so don't expect a fix or support overnight (although this often happens). Making sense of BDD and sharing it with those around you is a long but highly worthwhile process that you will get better at with practice.

As Jerry Cantrell said, "Part of the healing process is sharing with other people who care."

Self-Monitoring: What is it?

You've made an incredible amount of progress in your healing journey so far, getting clear on what your unique experience of BDD looks like, understanding yourself better, and learning how to use several powerful tools and exercises to continue to move forward.

I'll be sharing more of these in the final chapters of this book so you can support your physical, mental, and emotional health, feel empowered and confident, and make your body image issues a thing of the past.

But before I do this, I want to quickly check in with you and share another tool that can help guide you through the rest of this journey and ensure you're always heading in the right direction.

You've moved from that dark and scary place you were once in and climbed that mountain so you could gain a better perspective on the journey ahead. Then, fully equipped with the right weapons and tools, you started to fight your way through that BDD wilderness, defeating many demons along the way.

Now, I want you to pause and reflect on how far you've come so far. I want you to check your imaginary map and review where you are, what obstacles you may still face, and how you can continue to defeat them.

The most effective way to do this is by self-monitoring.

Why self-monitoring?

By watching your thoughts, emotions, body feelings and behaviors at this point, you can better understand how you think and how it affects your feelings and behaviors in every aspect of your life. You'll develop even more skills to manage and overcome your difficulties so you can tackle anything that life throws at you.

Even if you feel that you don't need to take this step, I highly encourage you to do it. You may believe that you have made significant progress in your healing but there may still be subconscious factors that can fester and worsen if you don't give them the attention they need—this could push you right back to where you started.

Self-monitoring will involve tracking three key elements:

- Your thoughts

- Your mood

- Your behaviors

Tracking your thoughts

As you learned back in Chapter 3, you are separate from those obsessive negative thoughts that plague your existence and cause you to doubt yourself.

You learned how things like changing your mindset, identifying your goals, discovering your values, and creating a positive environment could help you overcome these thoughts and break free from their grip.

Now you know that you can challenge these thoughts, assumptions, and habits and help stop those cognitive distortions that leave you feeling that you're ugly or flawed as a human being.

So the next step I want you to take is to start taking note of these thoughts, writing them down in your notebook or journal, and challenging them as they appear.

When you do this, you might be surprised at what you hear. When I got to this point, I thought I'd reclaimed control. But this negativity ran much deeper than I'd realized.

By writing them down and fighting back, I was able to fix those catastrophizing thoughts and all-or-nothing thinking that were overwhelming my brain and shift even closer toward positivity. My responses then became the new, improved narrator in my life, strengthening my mental health and forcing the negative internal voice to take a backseat.

Here's how you can do the same:

1. Keep a notebook and pen, phone or laptop close by at all times.

2. Every time you have a negative thought, write down what it is along with the time of day, possible triggers, and how the thought made you feel (on a scale of 1 to 10, with 10 being the biggest impact.

3. Review these thoughts, and then challenge them by asking yourself the following questions:

- What evidence do I have that what I believe is actually true?

- **Am I confusing a thought with a fact?**

- Am I falling into a thinking trap (e.g., catastrophizing or all-or-nothing treatment)?

- What would I tell a friend if he/she had the same thought?

- Am I blaming myself for something which is not really my fault?

- Am I taking something personally which has little or nothing to do with me?

4. How could you reframe the thought? Write down your answers along with the thoughts you had and see what insight you gained.

If you do this every time, you will almost certainly be surprised at the thought itself and the insight it can give you.

Tracking your mood

Everyone's mood fluctuates throughout the day. One moment we can feel relatively happy and content with our lives, that we have everything under control, and that the future is positive. Then we can feel overwhelmed, stressed, upset, and get lost in a hole of negative, obsessive thoughts, and worry.

Our moods affect everything throughout our lives, from our relationship with ourselves to our relationships with others, our work life, our financial situation, and our overall happiness.

The only problem is that sometimes our moods feel like they've come completely out of the blue with no warning or explanation, so we don't recognize them as such or know what we can do to feel better.

If you start tracking your mood, you can identify any triggers, learn how lifestyle factors like diet, sleep, physical activity, and alcohol consumption can affect your mood, and develop healthier coping mechanisms.

There are various ways you can do this.

1. Daily journaling

This one is great if you already have a journaling practice or you'd prefer to minimize time spent on your phone. Simply grab your notebook, focus, and start writing the following observation:

- What is the name of the emotion?

- Did you notice a shift in your emotions?

- What do you think caused the emotion?

- What was happening around you when you felt the emotion?

- What were you thinking when you felt the emotion?

- How did you act or respond to the emotion?

- Is this response appropriate for the situation?

2. Mood tracker app

I'm a big fan of using mood tracker apps[15] because they're easy to use, can send you reminders, and you can simply pull your phone from your pocket and start recording your observations. My personal favorite is the CBT (cognitive behavioral therapy) Thought Diary because it uses tools for various therapeutic approaches, including CBT, ACT (acceptance and commitment therapy), and positive psychology to help you improve your mood. However, I recommend that you research several to find out which best suits your needs and budget. Most mood tracker apps are available from Apple Store and Google play. Here are my suggestions:

- CBT Thought Diary

- Daylio

- MyTherapy

- MoodKit

- MoodTracker

3. Mood chart

A mood chart is a visual tool you can use to track your emotions, usually using a grid that you can color to indicate how you are feeling that day. Many love this tool because it's a simple and effective tool to help you gain a better insight into BDD and develop better coping techniques.

Tracking your behavior

Finally, you should also ensure you're tracking your behaviors, especially those that are symptomatic of BDD. This could include mirror checking, skin picking, eating habits, or your social activities.

Start by identifying one behavior you'd like to check, then find a way to record these behaviors.

---

[15] Cherry, K. (2021, June 27). What is a mood tracker? Verywell Mind. Retrieved March 20, 2023, from https://www.verywellmind.com/what-is-a-mood-tracker-5119337

For example, you may choose to record them in your journal, notebook, phone, or by taking voice recordings.

Every time you notice yourself doing this particular behavior, make a note of it alongside any observations regarding your mood, potential triggers, thoughts, and how intense the urge to carry out this behavior was.

It's also a good idea to set yourself a regular schedule where you can check in and record any behaviors so you don't forget. This could include writing at a certain time of day, after a certain activity or at regular intervals.

By tracking your thoughts, mood, and behavior in this way, you'll gain greater insight into your current symptoms of BDD, learn which factors affect your mental health, and discover better coping techniques and tools for a happier, healthier future.

Summary

Taking control of your life, setting healthy boundaries and learning how to communicate your needs with others is key when it comes to healing from your BDD.

Of course, the magic won't happen overnight: it took me many months of practice before I was able to slip into a place of greater mental comfort and ease but it was certainly worth the effort.

Again, I recommend you complete any of the exercises you missed, then come back to rejoin me as I guide you through the self-love and self-compassion habits and practices that will become your go-to tools for emotional and physical support.

Chapter 5

A Healthier You Inside and Out

"Your body hears everything your mind says."

– Naomi Judd

You've come such a long way in your healing journey already! I hope you are as proud of yourself as I am. So, before we start this chapter, I want to congratulate you for being brave, facing those inner demons, and finding the strength to choose a better path for your mental, emotional, and physical health.

Up until this point, you've learned more about BDD and explored what your unique experience of this mental health problem is, learned how to create a positive environment for healing, and then started to set boundaries, monitor your habits and open up the conversation with those who love and care about you.

These are the very same self-development tools that I used to kickstart what I used to call my 'Freedom Project' and lay those strong and healthy foundations I could lean on during my battle with BDD and healing journey.

In this chapter, I'll be focusing more closely on ways we can adopt a positive view of ourselves and the world around us by focusing on gratitude. Then I'll explain the role that self-esteem plays in how you feel and your healing journey and share some simple, healthy, and fun ways you can develop a better sense of self, boost your self-esteem, and find your sense of purpose. Let's dive straight in!

Develop a gratitude practice

Gratitude[16] is the act of feeling thankful and happy about the positive things in our life.

Depending on where you are in your healing journey, you are most likely rolling your eyes as I write these words, thinking that you don't have anything in your life to be thankful for. Your life has been plagued with negative obsessive thoughts, self-disgust, and suffering lately, so what do you have to be grateful for?

According to scientists, this is part of the problem.

When we suffer from BDD, anxiety, or depressive thinking, we focus on these problem areas in our life and allow them to overshadow everything else. Or we catastrophize and jump to the worst-case scenario when we look to the future, believing that our thoughts are a reflection of reality.

Even though we know that picking away at this scab of negativity will leave us feeling even worse, we can't help doing it. Our negative thoughts keep us trapped in this cycle that, when fed, continues to grow stronger.

If you can develop a gratitude practice, you can start to wriggle free of the grip of negative thinking and discover that, yes, even if you are suffering from a mental health problem or have incredible stress, pain, or even trauma in your life, you still have a lot to be thankful for.

You'll start noticing the birds singing outside your window at sunrise. Appreciate the smile of excitement on a child's face. Feel a wave of pleasure as you enjoy a loving conversation with a friend or partner, bite into a delicious strawberry, or relish in the feeling of warm sunshine on your face.

By starting to notice these simple pleasures, you'll start training your brain to notice and appreciate more of them, breaking free from negative thoughts and changing your perspective.

If you continue to practice gratitude, you'll continue to notice more positive things in the world and boost your happiness, life satisfaction, and health whilst also helping BDD, anxiety, depression, and even anger to release you from their grip.

---

[16] Cherry, K. (2021, October 29). What is gratitude? Verywell Mind. Retrieved March 20, 2023, from https://www.verywellmind.com/what-is-gratitude-5206817

With this tool, we can better handle stress, sleep better, have higher self-esteem and lower blood pressure, and start feeling good about our lives and our bodies, realizing that there is so much more to life than worrying about our appearance.

Yes, I know that it can feel almost impossible to see positivity when all you see are your perceived flaws, negative thoughts, and pain. I certainly scoffed the first time I heard about gratitude. But I decided that it was worth trying. After all, what did I have to lose?

Step by step, I was able to take control of my perspective of the world and start to feel happy again. It's been a total game-changer for me and it will be for you, too, if you only give it a try.

How does a gratitude practice work?

I'll be honest, when I heard about gratitude practices, I immediately thought it was some weird hippie thing. But as I did my research, I discovered that science shows that it does help shift our mindsets and free ourselves from toxic thoughts and emotions, helping us to live happier and more fulfilling lives. It's even more effective when used alongside other mental health tools such as therapy, journaling, CBT, and meditation, making it perfect for us BDD sufferers.

In one study[17], researchers found that gratitude has a long-lasting effect on the brain and helps us to feel more positive in the future, even if we don't share it. Study participants who expressed gratitude enjoyed a long-term improvement in their mental health, even months after the study ended.

If you start a gratitude practice, you'll have an effective tool that will help live a happier life well into the future. Of course, this takes time, especially when you're working hard to keep those negative thoughts and toxic inner voices under control.

Nevertheless, by doing it, we can learn to love our lives, appreciate everything around us, and be grateful for more than just the human body.

---

[17]   Joshua Brown Joshua Brown, Brown, J. B. J., & Wong, J. W. J. (n.d.). How gratitude changes you and your brain. Greater Good. Retrieved March 20, 2023, from https://greatergood.berkeley.edu/article/item/how_gratitude_changes_you_and_your_brain

How to use gratitude to overcome BDD

1. Start a gratitude journal

The most effective way to foster a sense of gratitude in your life is to start with a gratitude practice. Find a time every day when you won't be disturbed (such as first thing in the morning), and write down five things that you feel grateful for. That's it.

You can write anything you want, no matter how big or small. During the early days of my practice, I wrote down tiny things like...

- I am grateful to be breathing.

- I am grateful for the sunshine this morning.

- I am grateful for waking up a few seconds before my alarm.

- I am grateful to feel rested.

- I am grateful for a warm bed in winter.

2. Start the day positively

The mornings can be one of the most challenging times of the day when you're suffering from a mental health problem such as BDD. It's like someone poured gasoline on the fire of obsessive thoughts, and negativity swirls around your brain, growing stronger with every second that passes.

If you start the day with these negative emotions, they'll set the stage for the rest of the day and it will be difficult to shift your mindset and perspective.

That's why I recommend that you take a few moments in the morning to feel gratitude and write in your gratitude journal so you can start the day on a positive note.

3. Focus on the positive

Throughout your day, you should also keep your mind open to the positives in life, become aware of them, and then breathe in their beauty and joy. This will help you avoid thinking of the negatives and see any challenges as opportunities or chances for learning. You'll also develop a more positive mindset and have something to write in your gratitude journal in the morning!

4. Live in the present

With BDD, we often get caught up in our bodies and thoughts, unable to connect with the world and fully appreciate what is happening around us. Instead, be fully present in the moment, engaging all of your senses whilst staying aware of your emotions and thoughts.

Practices like meditation and yoga can be very helpful here (more on this later). I also highly recommend you read the book 'The Power of Now' by Eckhart Tolle[18]—I believe it will change your life.

When you can focus on yourself like this, you can rediscover your happiness and begin to thank your body for keeping you alive, not criticize it for having a 'flaw'.

Improve your self-esteem

Self-esteem[19] is how you feel about and value yourself. If you can recognize your strengths, believe you have value as a person, can show yourself kindness, try new things, believe you deserve happiness, and can move past mistakes without blaming yourself, you have healthy self-esteem.

But if you suffer from BDD, your self-esteem is likely to be at rock bottom or close to non-existent. You believe that you're unlovable or worthless because of your perceived flaw and might even believe that having a terminal disease would be better than having to live with your 'flaw' every day.

The situation is compounded because BDD could be causing your self-esteem issues, and your self-esteem issues could be worsening BDD.

I'd suffered from low self-esteem throughout my entire life, or so it felt. I could only remember feeling 'less than' other people around me or often feeling that someone would find out that I was inherently flawed as a human being or incompetent if they knew the real me. I felt lost and broken.

---

[18]   Tolle, E., & Tolle, E. (2016). Practicing the power of now: Essential teachings, meditations, and exercises from the power of now. Amazon. Retrieved March 20, 2023, from https://www.amazon.com/Power-Now-Eckhart-Tolle/dp/B0095GVWMA

[19]   What is self-esteem? Mind. (n.d.). Retrieved March 20, 2023, from https://www.mind.org.uk/information-support/types-of-mental-health-problems/self-esteem/about-self-esteem/

Then that toxic inner voice would only reinforce my beliefs, telling me that yes, I was indeed unlovable and flawed. I only had to look at my appearance in the mirror for confirmation of this painful fact.

It was only when I started my gratitude practice that I realized how difficult things had become and how low my self-esteem had sunk. It was close to impossible to find anything to write on my gratitude list, let alone find the motivation to pick up the pen in the first place.

But then I read a line about self-esteem and BDD that shifted my perspective and showed me where I needed to focus next if I wanted to continue to heal. It was this:

"Too often people with BDD think that their appearance has to improve before they can sufficiently engage in these types of pursuits. Think again. If you wait for that, the BDD will win every time." [20]

These sentences sparked a new fire inside me. There was no way that I wanted BDD to win, so I was willing to do whatever it took to boost my self-esteem and rediscover happiness. Not only did I start my gratitude practice in earnest then, but I also looked into effective ways to improve my self-esteem.

How do we build our self-esteem?

Unfortunately, there's no magic pill we can take to raise our self-esteem so we can start to feel good about ourselves and loosen the grip that BDD has on us.

But there are several cognitive behavioral therapy tricks we can use to help us challenge those negative thoughts, break the patterns, build our sense of self-worth, and look towards the future with positivity. I worked through each of these in my own journey and I know you will find them powerful.

Here are the steps I used to boost my self-esteem so that BDD could start to loosen its grip on my life and I could start to move towards happiness and fulfillment.

1. Look in the mirror

This may sound contradictory because up until now, I've been advising you

20   "Am I ok today?" - BDD and the role of self-esteem. BDD. (n.d.). Retrieved March 20, 2023, from https://bdd.iocdf.org/expert-opinions/am-i-ok-today-bdd-and-the-role-of-self-esteem/

gainst mirror-checking. But this is different, and you will soon discover what mean.

First, make a decision to look in the mirror and challenge your thoughts about your appearance. Before you do, pause and take a moment to check what thoughts come to mind. These might be, *"I hope I don't look disgusting today,"* or *'I hope I'm ok,"* or worse, *"OMG, I'm going to look so ugly I'll be unable to shift my awareness from that flaw"*.

Whatever comes up, I want you to write it down. Then start to consider where this comes from.

Is this really about your flaw, or is it about the way you're feeling inside? Are you really hoping you FEEL ok, and not that you LOOK ok? Do you really feel disgusted by your perceived flaw, or are you really worried that people won't love and accept you because of it?

Note: Whether or not you choose to look into the mirror is totally up to you. In fact, I often recommend that people don't if they believe it will feed their BDD. But the point is that you are doing this to become more aware of your thought processes so you can challenge them.

2. Make note of your negative thoughts as they happen

Many of our toxic thoughts can appear seemingly out of nowhere throughout the day. One moment we can be discussing an interesting topic with a friend, then the next, we can feel crushed by these thoughts and our overall low self-esteem.

You can challenge and regain your sense of control if you write down what they are and then respond to them. For example, if that negative voice tells you that you're stupid, write it down, then consider.

- What evidence do you have that contradicts that statement?

- What would your friends say?

- What are you good at that proves that you're not stupid?

Write this down too. Then repeat the process whenever these thoughts appear.

3. Create a positivity list

You have more value in this world than you think right now. You have so many talents, skills, and love to offer the world, and you need to start remembering what they are.

By creating a positivity list, you'll help challenge those negative thoughts that come up quickly and easily and set a solid foundation for healthy self-esteem well into the future.

To do this, simply grab a notepad and write down positive things about yourself. I recommend you start with at least five positives and add as many more as you can think of, adding to it often.

If you're struggling, ask family and friends for their input too. Then display this list somewhere you'll see it often, such as on your fridge or in the bathroom, or use it as a screensaver on your phone or computer.

4. Break the pattern

Next time you're self-critical, pause and, instead, choose to be gentle with yourself. Ask yourself what you would say to a friend if they were in that same situation, then apply it to yourself.

This can help you become your own 'inner parent' and develop a calm place of acceptance within that can help you rebuild your self-esteem. Write this down in your journal if you want to further strengthen your fight against BDD.

5. Celebrate your successes

When you have a quiet moment, pause, and consider what you've achieved throughout your life, no matter how big or small.

What was it you achieved? What challenges did you have to overcome to achieve it? How has it benefited your life today?

This could include passing an exam, being an excellent parent or friend, traveling the world, or even how far you've come in your healing journey already. By doing so, you'll reinforce both the positives in your life and your sense of self-esteem.

6. Build positive relationships

As I mentioned in Chapter 3, you are the sum of the five people closest to you. That's why it's so important to build positive relationships with people who appreciate you, are kind, and can provide you with the support you need.

If there are negative people in your life, reconsider whether you want them around or get clear on your boundaries (as we read in Chapter 4),and then communicate with them. This can often help improve a relationship so you can keep good people close without having to ditch friends who have made mistakes.

7. Challenge yourself

Building healthy self-esteem can't happen if you hide away in your home, afraid of the world and afraid of yourself. It's only by challenging ourselves to break out of our comfort zone that we can start to believe in our personal power and value and start to celebrate our wins for a more positive mindset.

Why not look back to Chapter 3, where I talk about goal setting, and choose a goal to set yourself, no matter how small? When you achieve this goal (which you will!), you will give your self-esteem a boost and can move even further in your healing journey.

8. Use self-love affirmations

Self-love affirmations are a fantastic way to show yourself self-love and build your self-esteem. They're also easy to slot into your day, for example, while you're getting ready in the morning, driving in your car, when you use the bathroom, or at any other routine point during your day. They can significantly shift your mindset.

So, what are self-love affirmations? They're simply positive statements that you say to yourself.

Even though this idea may also sound slightly "hippie", there's scientific proof that self-love affirmations actually work, especially if you say them aloud. By doing so, you're sending a positive message of love to your brain, and you will start believing that they are true.

To get started, think of a few affirmations that really resonate with you. Here are some suggestions:[21]

- I am enough.

- I unconditionally love and accept myself.

- I am loved.

---

[21] Lucile Hernandez Rodriguez. (2022, November 11). 20 positive self love affirmations you'll want to do daily. Lucile Hernandez Rodriguez. Retrieved March 20, 2023, from https://www.lucilehr.com/blog/positive-self-love-af-firmations-youll-want-to-do-daily

- I completely forgive and accept myself.

- I have everything I need within myself.

- Showing up and doing my best every single day is already so much.

- I enjoy taking care of myself as much as taking care of others.

- I choose to love myself at every step of my journey.

- I am at peace with my past and future and choose to focus on the present moment.

- I am the source of my own happiness.

- I am grateful for everything that I am.

- I already am who I need to be.

- I am becoming the person I want to be.

- I release the need to judge myself and others.

- I treat myself like I would treat a friend.

- I am compassionate and loving towards myself.

- The only approval I need is my own.

- I release the need to judge myself negatively.

- I choose to speak lovingly about myself.

- I let my inner wisdom guide me to self-love.

Once you've chosen the ones you'll be using, make them your own by customizing them and adding whatever details you want. Then repeat them throughout your day, taking time to feel and accept the words as you do so.

Practice often, and you'll soon see a difference.

Practice often, and you'll soon see a difference.

"Healing yourself is connected with healing others."

– Yoko Ono

Find purpose

"Discovering your purpose is the most significant thing you will do in your life, and you, your loved ones, and the world will be better off because you went on this journey."

These wise words come from best-selling author and key performance coach, Mastin Kipp[22], who helps people create rapid change, connect to who they really are, and learn to live their lives with passion and purpose.

When I read his book, I knew that I wouldn't be the only one to benefit from his science-driven, life-changing approach because it makes sense. We all find ourselves wondering why we've been put on this planet, whether we suffer from BDD or not.

It's what has guided humans towards philosophy and religion for thousands of years as they wonder what is the point of this all. Why are we here? What is our unique purpose as human beings?

Science suggests that this evolved in us so that we can cooperate and achieve big things together, helping us to survive as a species. This may also be why having this sense of purpose is connected with better mental health, physical health, and happiness.

If you can identify your purpose, you can further build your sense of self-esteem and feel that your existence is truly worthwhile. You'll also help shift your focus away from your external appearance, take control of that negative inner voice, and feel like you're in control of your life. Best of all, you'll also start to feel much happier, sleep better, enjoy better mental health, better relationships, and greater financial prosperity.

---

[22] Create a healthy nervous system and thrive no matter what. Mastin Kipp. (2022, December 19). Retrieved March 20, 2023, from https://mastinkipp.com/

Your purpose doesn't have to be anything grand, like changing the world or discovering a vaccine that will help save humanity from the next pandemic. It can be anything that is meaningful to you, such as a hobby you love, travel, meeting people with kindness, spending time with people you love, following your passion, and so on.

How to find your purpose

Finding your purpose might seem tricky when you're overwhelmed with negative thoughts and the future seems anything but bright.

But hopefully, by the time you read these words, you've already worked hard to set the foundations for better mental health and are already practicing several of the tools and tips I've shared so far. Either way, working through the following exercises can help you gain clarity on what your purpose could be, not only helping you overcome your negative thoughts, boost your self-esteem, and achieve happiness but also giving you a better sense of your path for the future.

1. Think about what you care about.

What do you care about? Grab a notebook and write whatever comes to mind. If you're finding this hard, consider the following prompts.

- What are you good at?

- What skill do you have that can be used for a cause?

- What do you care about in your community?

- What would you do if you had a magic wand (or unlimited money) and could change anything?

2. Consider doing a values questionnaire

Although we already defined our values in Chapter 3, it can be helpful to work through one or several of the questionnaires that have been used in psychological research studies to help people spark change in their lives.

These go into more depth than what we've already covered, and I think you are ready for them at this point.

They are:

- Valued Living Questionnaire[23]

- Portrait Values Questionnaire[24]

- Personal Values Questionnaire[25]

Choose one and give it a try!

3. Recognize your strengths and talents

Next, spend some time considering what your personal strengths and talents are so you can think about how to apply them in your life. Ask yourself:

- What am I particularly good at?

- What do I really enjoy?

- How do I think I'll leave my mark on the world?

If you need help, it can be really useful to do the VIA Character Strengths Survey[26], which helps guide you through the process.

4. Try volunteering

Once you've gained some clarity on your strengths, why not experiment with them by volunteering for an organization focused on what you care about? This can help you understand whether this is indeed your purpose in life, encourage you to try new things and make a difference while also becoming part of something bigger than yourself and feeling needed in a way that has nothing to do with your physical appearance.

Simply search online for volunteer projects that you care about and give it a go!

---

[23] https://www.div12.org/wp-content/uploads/2015/06/Valued-Living-Questionnaire.pdf

[24] https://datadatabase.files.wordpress.com/2011/03/schwartz-value-inventory.pdf

[25] https://survey.valuescentre.com/ survey.html?id=5l1OmCPgJO6F-GafKLmkogR4E3lIuZOgB0EGag0Ki1CIOvC8MbC5eSA

[26] https://www.viacharacter.org/survey/account/register

5. Imagine your future self

Finally, take some time to imagine what your life could be like in 10, 20 or 30 years when you have overcome BDD, followed your purpose and if money wasn't an issue. What will you be doing? What will be important to you? What do you really care about and why? This is another great exercise to incorporate into your journaling practice and can help guide your recovery journey, giving you something positive to aim for in the future.

Reconnect with nature

Surprisingly, nature is vital to human mental, emotional, psychological, and physical health.

It helps us get the fresh air, sunshine, and exercise we need to be healthy, connects us with something larger than ourselves, and gives us a great opportunity to feel gratitude for the small things in life. After all, there's nothing quite as awe-inspiring and mood-boosting as seeing a beautiful view of a forest, faraway mountain, or the ocean.

Being outside can also boost our serotonin levels (the hormone connected to mood and mental health) and regulate our body clocks, so we sleep better, feel more rested, and enjoy better overall health.

If we can connect with the natural world, we can escape from the chaos of everyday life, feel more grounded, and stop being so aware of our physical appearance. This doesn't mean you need to pack up and go and live in the forest or go backpacking through the wilderness to feel the effects. Even a short walk outside in a park, woodland, or forest, listening to birdsong outside, swimming in a local river or lake, or indulging in a spot of gardening can provide the same benefits.

How to enjoy more green time

If we suffer from BDD and find social situations difficult, we are even more likely to stay inside, which leads to a disconnect from the natural world around us. If you can get more 'green time' you will significantly support your healing journey and find that you feel better faster.

Start small and aim to spend at least 10 minutes in nature or appreciating nature every day. For example, wake up 10 minutes earlier so you have time to listen to the birdsong or appreciate the sunrise before your day starts. If you have a job or are in education, head outside for a walk in the local park at lunchtime. Or consider going for a weekly nature walk in your local park, nature reserve, beach, or forest somewhere.

Even if the weather isn't great, you can still go outside. Just find clothes that will keep you warm, and dry or protect you from the sun and get out there!

Summary

In this chapter, we've worked on building your self-esteem, fostering a sense of positivity and gratitude, and learning more about yourself through questionnaires designed to help you identify your values, strengths, and talents.

I've shared the same techniques I used in my own healing journey that will help reinforce that inner strength and show you the path you can take to live a rich and fulfilling life.

Chapter 6

Connecting Deeply with Yourself

"Wherever you go, there you are."

- Jon Kabat-Zinn

I'd like to start this chapter by sharing a personal story with you so you can see whether you relate. It's about emotions, and, more specifically, how I dealt with those difficult thoughts and feelings that used to flood my awareness.

Like most stories relating to feelings, it starts back when I was a child and living with a mother who suffered from severe bouts of depression. Seemingly out of the blue, there would be days when she'd struggle to get out of bed, would seem emotionally disconnected from me and my siblings, and then blow up in anger if I mentioned even the tiniest thing, such as wanting to go to the park to play. It was my fault. I was making unreasonable demands. She felt trapped and upset by the suggestion that she wasn't being a 'good mother' and would simply withdraw.

As you'd expect, I learned to deal with this as best as I could. Emotions were something to be feared and hidden away. Any problems were mine to deal with, and, deep down, I was scared that any emotions would push through and force me to mention them.

It was my childhood coping mechanism. But as with many other coping mechanisms, this continued throughout my life, and I developed new coping mechanisms to deal with the challenges life brought me. I believe that this was at the root of my BDD and all the other unhealthy behaviors I adopted over the years.

When I finally realized that my symptoms of BDD were controlling my life and I started to open myself up to these emotions, no matter how hard, found freedom. I was no longer scared of what these feelings were telling me and learned how to reconnect with my inner world, accept these feelings and work through them. It was totally liberating on all levels.

I'm almost certain that you suffer from the same problem or, at least, bury your own emotions. After all, it's unlikely you would have suffered from body image problems if it wasn't for this.

That's why, in this chapter, I want you to stop running away or hiding from these emotions and instead learn how to recognize, accept, and move through them. The best tools we can use for this are mindfulness, meditation, and reiki. Let's work through each of these in turn.

Learn the art of mindfulness

Do you ever find that your mind is invaded by thoughts that are going a million miles per hour? No matter how much you try to slow them down, it can often feel like they gather momentum and leave you feeling even more anxious, stressed, and overwhelmed than you did before.

This is very normal when you suffer from BDD, stress, or anxiety. I remember that at my lowest point, I would lie in bed, totally exhausted from the day. I'd followed all those recommended self-care techniques and felt relatively relaxed.

Yet as soon as my head hit the pillow, I'd begin to feel like a hostage of my own anxious thoughts and negative inner voice. It was as if they knew I was at my most vulnerable and chose that moment to intensify their attack. I felt desperate, continually unable to get the good night's sleep I knew I needed, but clueless when it came to what to do.

Of course, this wasn't the only time that the negative voices would choose to attack. Often, they came completely out of the blue, triggered by something from my subconscious that I had no awareness of until I was pushed back into that desperate mental space.

Then one day, I came across mindfulness[27] —the practice of becoming fully present, aware of where we are and what we are doing, and not overwhelmed or reactive to what is happening around us.

---

[27] Staff, M. (2023, January 6). What is mindfulness? Mindful. Retrieved March 30, 2023, from https://www.mindful.org/what-is-mindfulness/

The experts[28] said that by learning this ancient technique, I could free myself from these racing thoughts, ease my stress and anxiety, sleep better, feel happier, and potentially ease my BDD.

When I first heard about it, I admit that I rolled my eyes and decided that there was no way that it would help me. I'd already tried everything to stop these negative thoughts and felt that 'emptying my mind' was an impossible task to accomplish.

But as I discovered, mindfulness isn't about emptying your mind, ignoring your thoughts and feelings, or switching your brain off (because that simply doesn't work). Instead, it's about connecting with the moment and allowing those thoughts to be recognized and processed in a healthy way so that you can release yourself from their clutches.

More importantly, it made a huge difference to how much control my thoughts had over me and was key to helping me accept myself as I was and free myself from BDD.

The energy of mindfulness

Before I explain what mindfulness looks like and how you can practice it, I want to explain more about how it can help you to overcome BDD.

As we discussed in earlier chapters, BDD is often triggered because of trauma or difficult experiences that take place throughout your life. Even if you don't realize it, these experiences often get buried deep inside our subconscious and shape both our thoughts and our experience of life.

We're too scared to face them, so look for ways to distract ourselves so we don't have to suffer through the pain. This can often involve zoning out in front of the TV or social media, using drugs or alcohol, smoking too much, engaging in casual sex, or even developing anxiety disorders that fool us into believing we're in control.

These unhealthy habits may seem to work temporarily, but the trauma is still there, just beneath the surface, shouting louder and louder to catch our attention. The longer we ignore the message, the worse the problem becomes.

However, mindfulness can help us become aware of our subconscious, allow

---

[28]   Mindfulness may improve body dissatisfaction and body dysmorphic ... (n.d.). Retrieved March 30, 2023, from https://inkblotuoft.files.wordpress.com/2016/09/janice-to.pdf

that inner trauma to be heard and help us naturally process what has happened. It can also help us survive those moments of crisis where we feel like those negative thoughts have become totally out of control, without intensifying our suffering.

How mindfulness works

When we speak about our minds, we're referring to two different parts: the conscious mind and the subconscious mind.

Our conscious mind (active awareness) is the part that we are aware of and can be controlled with our attention, focusing on our breathing, and so on.

Our subconscious mind (also known as root consciousness) is where our past experiences are stored and where we learn and process information. When you ride a bike, drive a car, or feel triggered by an experience, it comes from your subconscious mind. It's also where our past feelings and emotions are stored, including anger, hurt, sorrow, joy, and trauma. These can become like seeds, waiting to be watered by the conscious mind and emerge into our awareness, triggering those difficult feelings.

However, mindfulness is also a seed that lives in our conscious mind and can be called upon whenever we wish so we can recognize their presence and take care of them, without forcing them back inside.

Every time we touch the seed of mindfulness, we can breathe and say hello to our feelings, soothe ourselves, and relieve the internal pressure that drives our inner trauma and feeds BDD.

How to practice mindfulness

The good news is that mindfulness isn't a difficult skill to learn and master. In fact, we all have this natural ability to create space for ourselves to think, breathe, nurture ourselves, and create inner peace.

It's completely free, you don't need to buy anything, and you don't need to quieten your mind. Simply by focusing on the present moment, letting those thoughts arise without judgment, and accepting them, you can become more mindful.

Of course, your thinking-conscious brain is likely to try to take over and those negative thoughts may try to take over. In fact, it almost certainly will. But if you allow them to be heard, avoid judgment, then return your attention to the present moment, they will stop fighting for your attention and will eventually ɔosen their grip on your life.

Ready? Here's how to do it[29]:

1. Sit quietly in a place where you won't be disturbed.

2. Set a timer for five or 10 minutes.

3. Pay attention to your breath as it flows in and out of your body, without trying to control it.

4. Notice when your mind has wandered and bring it back to the breath.

Self-love and meditation

You may have noticed that there's a similarity between mindfulness practices and meditation,[30] and often the two terms are used interchangeably.

However, the difference is that mindfulness can be practiced anywhere and involves bringing your attention to the present moment, whereas meditation is a more specific seated practice where you use focus to turn inwards to feel calm, increase inner peace, and increase your overall awareness.

The two also complement each other perfectly, which is why I also added a self-love meditation practice to my healing toolbox.

Why self-love meditation?

You are beautifully unique. There is no one like you in the whole world and you are simply irreplaceable.

When you are living with the burden of BDD, this thought can feel unbearable and leave you feeling like you are horribly abnormal, different, or somehow defective.

---

29   Staff, M. (2022, October 4). How to practice mindfulness. Mindful. Retrieved March 30, 2023, from https://www.mindful.org/how-to-practice-mindfulness/

30   What is meditation? Headspace. (n.d.). Retrieved March 30, 2023, from https://www.headspace.com/meditation-101/what-is-meditation

But if you can learn to foster your sense of self-love and view your uniqueness in a positive light, you can transform the way you think and feel, boosting your self-esteem and confidence in the process.

Imagine what this would look like in your life. You could become more compassionate towards yourself, stop comparing yourself to others, learn to love your body for the miracle that it is, focus on joy and discover what true contentment means. You'll stop being so self-critical, naturally reduce your anxiety, depression, or symptoms of BDD, and see challenges in life as a temporary state, not a life sentence.

Self-love meditation can be a game-changer.

How to use self-love meditation

There are many different types of meditation that you can try to help ease your BDD, relieve stress and tension, free yourself from negative thoughts, and build your self-confidence, self-worth, and inner strength. This includes:

- Mindfulness meditation

- Spiritual meditation

- Focused meditation

- Movement meditation

- Mantra meditation

- Transcendental meditation

- Progressive relaxation

- Loving-kindness meditation

However, I found that the most effective type for me was self-love meditation because it allowed me to gain real insight into my thought patterns, understand that my thoughts were separate from myself, and learn to love myself. I also used self-love affirmations to nurture this self-love and find greater inner peace.

Here's how to do it:

1. Find a comfortable place to rest, either sitting or lying down.

2. Focus on your breath without trying to control or judge it.

3. Notice any emotions that might appear, then feel where this emotion is located in your body. Perhaps you feel it in your throat? In your stomach? In your chest?

4. Notice any thoughts that accompany this emotion without trying to silence or change them.

5. Repeat one of the following affirmations to yourself:

- "I see you [name your emotion]. That sounds really hard; I'm sorry."

- "I'm here. Stay as long as you like [name your emotion], you're welcome here."

- "I see you [name your emotion]. I love you."

- Notice whether you have any resistance to these above statements and try to intensify the feelings of love to outshine the negative.

If you'd prefer to follow a guided self-love meditation, I highly recommend you download either the Calm or Headspace app or try this free self-love meditation on YouTube.[31] I also invite you to explore my audiobooks on BDD found on Audible.

---

[31]   YouTube. (2022, March 8). 10-minute guided meditation: Self-love | Self. YouTube. Retrieved March 30, 2023, from https://www.youtube.com/watch?v=vj0JDwQLof4

Breathwork for self-love

Another great way to cultivate self-love and compassion is with breathwork which you can pair with meditation or simply practice on your own. (*Note: Before you start, please speak to a healthcare professional to ensure you are safe to practice*).

As you may have noticed in this chapter, focusing on our breath is key to fostering feelings of calm and peace and can ease suffering.[32] This is because our breathing patterns are connected to our nervous systems. When you encounter a frightening or threatening situation (whether exterior or interior), the speed of your breath naturally increases, signaling to the body to continue its fight or flight stress response. Similarly, when you feel calm, your breath slows, and you enjoy a sense of contentment and release that soothes your nervous system.

Back when I was starting my healing journey, I noticed that by simply focusing on my breath, I could ease that sense of overwhelm and panic that would often overcome me and slow my negative thoughts. I was also able to reconnect with my inner self, stop comparing myself to others or look for external validation, and feed the love within.

This surprised me. I'd always believed that taking a few deep breaths or focusing on my breath was nonsense and ineffective or something that only Zen masters and hippies concerned themselves with. But over time, I noticed that breathing could dilute negativity, help me resolve the issue, and learn to trust myself.

How should you practice breathwork for BDD?

At the start, I simply focused on my breath and allowed those difficult feelings to be heard and then dissipate. But as I did more research, I discovered that there are seventeen different breathwork techniques[33] that offer different benefits. These include:

---

[32]   Breathwork for Self Love. Samantha Story MS, L.Ac. (n.d.). Retrieved March 30, 2023, from https://www.samanthastory.com/events/2019/10/20/breathwork-for-self-love
[33]   17 breathwork techniques to improve your physical & mental health. (n.d.). Retrieved March 30, 2023, from https://www.othership.us/resources/breathwork-techniques

1. Box breathing

This technique focuses on taking slow deep breaths and is often used for stress reduction and improved performance.

To practice, inhale through your nose for a count of four, hold for another four, exhale through your mouth for four, then hold for the final count of four. Repeat as needed.

2. Diaphragmatic breathing

Also known as belly breathing, this technique is great for relaxation, stress reduction, easing anxiety, depression, and mental health problems, and improving concentration.

To practice, place one hand on your upper chest and one on your stomach between your ribs and diaphragm. Breathe in through your nose and fill your entire belly area with air. Exhale, then repeat as desired.

3. Pursed lip breathing

This technique is great for helping you to improve your lung strength and brings fresh, rejuvenating air into your body.

To practice, breathe in through your nose for a count of two. Then purse your lips and breath out slowly to a count of four. Repeat as desired.

4. 4-7-8 Breathing

Another stress-relieving technique, this one helps ease anxiety and tension, boosts your mood, and improves sleep.

To practice, inhale through your mouth to a count of four. Then hold your breath for a count of seven and breathe out through your mouth to a count of eight. Repeat as desired.

5. Breath focus technique

This technique is simply mindful breathing that can help you boost feelings of happiness, relaxation, and calm.

To practice, pay attention to the way you're breathing without trying to change it. Then consider switching between breathing normally and deep breathing. Repeat as required.

7. Equal breathing

Also known as 'circular breathing,' this exercise helps you to relieve stress and anxiety quickly by calming your nervous system.

To practice, simply sit quietly and breathe in and out through your nose. Count to ensure the breaths are the same length, and repeat as desired.

8. Resonant breathing

This is another simple exercise that can boost your mood and improve your heart rate. To do it, simply breathe in for a count of five and breathe out for a count of five. Repeat as desired.

9. Holotropic breathwork

Holotropic breathwork is a New Age practice that can help you release negative emotions and is best learned with a trained expert.

10. Shamanic breathwork

This is a spiritual breathing technique that can help you heal quickly and easily. Again, it's best learned with a professional.

11. Rebirthing breathwork

Rebirthing breathwork can help promote joy and peace and help you access your deepest thoughts and desires. Look for a course or private in-person session to learn.

12. Pranayama breathwork

Also known as yoga breathing, pranayama breathwork is a variety of techniques that help clear mental and physical blockages and can help relieve stress and anxiety, increase focus, and increase your energy.

13. SOMA breathwork

SOMA breathwork helps to improve your overall breathing to help balance your nervous system, boost healing, help you manage stress, and release negative emotions. Look online to find a SOMA breathwork class near you.

14. Neurodynamic breathwork

A continuation of holotropic breathwork, neurodynamic breathwork helps people connect with their higher self and gain control over their emotions. Again, it's best learned in a class.

15. Somatic breath therapy

Somatic breath therapy is a type of breathing designed to increase your oxygen levels, recover from trauma, reduce stress, and enjoy better sleep. Look for a private session, group session, or workshop near you for the best results.

16. Transformational breathwork

Transformational breathwork can help reduce stress and anxiety and release negativity. Similar to holotropic and rebirthing breathwork, it's better learned from an expert.

17. Vivation

Vivation combines elements of yoga, tantra, and meditation to help you release negative thoughts, manage additions and improve your relationships. You can find these classes online- simply search Google to find the right one for you.

As you can see, there are many different types of breathwork that can provide different benefits. However, if you want the best results, I recommend you read through the list above, choose one then give it a try. If you're a total beginner, start with the first seven on the list first.

Again, please check with a licensed medical professional before trying any of the breathwork techniques above.

Reiki for self-love

Have you ever heard of reiki or wondered what it is? Simply put, it involves using energy healing to bring our energies back into alignment.[34]

If you think back to your school days, you might remember that everything in our universe is made of energy. As American Scientist magazine said, "Each electron produces an electromagnetic field that extends throughout space.[35]"

These electrons are everywhere; therefore, energy is all around us, both in a physical and emotional sense.

Various philosophies have given different names to this energy throughout time, including Prana in Indian philosophies, Qi or Chi in Chinese traditions, Ki in Japan, Mana in Polynesia, Chu'lel in Mayan, and Universal Life Force in the Western world.

---

[34] Administrator, R. (2019, September 10). What is reiki? Reiki. Retrieved March 30, 2023, from https://www.reiki.org/faqs/what-reiki

[35] Translucidmind. (2020, February 28). What's everything made of? Translucidmind.com. Retrieved March 30, 2023, from https://translucidmind.com/whats-everything-made-of/

The practice of reiki uses this energy to heal imbalances from the inside out. Best of all, everyone can access this energy, starting from practicing simple breathwork and becoming more aware of how your energy moves and shifts through your body.

How to practice reiki for self-love

Start by rubbing your hands together and then placing them over your eyes to feel the heat.

While you're doing this, take some deep breaths in through your nose and out through your mouth, feeling love for yourself, your friends and family and the entire world. Then recite the following mantras.

- "Just for today, I will not feel anger."

- "Just for today, I will not worry."

- "I appreciate everything and give thanks."

- "I embody the teachings in action."

- "I am kind to myself and other beings."

You can also use these mantras throughout the day when needed.

Another powerful reiki self-love exercise is visualization. To practice this, find somewhere quiet to relax and close your eyes. Imagine white light filled with love traveling up through your spine to the crown of your head. Incorporate one of the breathing techniques into this visualization practice.

Get active!

It might surprise you to know that physical activity can be a fantastic way to reconnect with yourself and ease any difficult thoughts and emotions.

During my own healing journey, there was nothing more beneficial than lacing up my sneakers and going for a leisurely walk or jog. It gave me time to just be 'me' and process my thoughts and emotions. The activity left me feeling uplifted and positive when I returned. Even if it was just a ten-minute walk round the block, it helped me feel better.

Having said that, I knew that, as a BDD sufferer, I needed to be careful. There was no way I wanted to slip back into the unhealthy and destructive pattern of obsessive exercise that plagued me during the depths of my experience with BDD. That's why I started slowly, kept it simple, and avoided doing any vigorous exercise in the beginning.

Physical activity is known to be one of the most effective ways to ease anxiety, depression, and obsessive thoughts, boost your energy, reduce stress and tension, improve your confidence, and lift your mood. When you're recovering from BDD and you exercise, be sure to check your motives and set your intention—for now, you're doing this for your mind and overall wellbeing, not to change your body.

Why does physical activity work for BDD?

During exercise, feel-good chemicals (endorphins) are released into our brains and help us feel good physically, emotionally, and spiritually.

For us BDD sufferers, it also reminds us that our bodies are incredible feats of nature with a purpose.

Physical activity also gives us a sense of purpose, especially if we commit to a regular practice such as daily walks (and actually carry it out). This sense of achievement can continue to nourish our self-confidence and sense of self-worth, helping us move forward through our healing journey and view the future with greater confidence.

Ideally, we want to be getting active outdoors in natural spaces like beaches, parks, and places close to water. But any green space can be beneficial, even if that means walking around an urban area dotted with a few trees. It may be best to avoid exercising at the gym at the beginning of your healing journey because of the strong connection with the gym and the 'perfect body' image.

What should you do?

Any type of physical activity will help get those endorphins flowing and boost your mood, so look for something you love and try to do it as often as you can. Excellent options include walking, jogging, swimming, yoga, Pilates, and dancing.

Again, please be cautious when it comes to overexercising, as it can undo all the healing work you've done up to this point and cause a relapse. I recommend that you speak to your therapist or medical professional before you get started for more guidance.

Although the experts recommend that we should get around 150 minutes o moderate exercise per week, it's better to keep it short and low-impact in th beginning. Even a 10-minute walk can make a huge difference to how you fee In fact, when I notice that my mood is dipping, or resisting those compulsion feels hard, taking a quick walk is the best way to hit that reset button and gai some relief.

So, before we end this chapter, I want you to think about exercise. How coul you fit physical activity into your day? What would you like to do? What bring you joy? Once you've brainstormed a few ideas, choose one and then promise yourself you'll try. You'll be surprised at the difference it can make.

Summary

When we suffer from BDD, anxiety, or obsessive thoughts, we often try to bury our emotions because we're afraid of their power and want to gain relief from our symptoms. But as you learned in this chapter, it's only by accepting our emotions that we can identify the underlying causes and start to gently work through them.

We've seen how mindfulness, meditation, self-love practices, breathwork, reiki, and physical activity can be used throughout your day to deal with these challenging emotions and find inner peace, even when life feels unbearable.

Remember that it's completely normal to experience a range of emotions and that doesn't mean you have to be fearful of them. By accepting yourself, loving, and nurturing yourself, you too can break free from BDD.

Chapter 7

The New You

"You don't want to set yourself up for failure by replacing the thought with something that may not be realistic. A helpful technique could be to ask yourself what you would say to a friend in this situation."

— RACHEL GOLDMAN, PHD

I want to tell you that you have achieved amazing things by reading up until this final chapter in this book.

Even if you haven't put any of the tools and techniques I've shared into practice, you're now more aware of the factors that influence your 'internal weather', the fact that your thoughts and feelings are separate, and even learned how you can use self-care and daily practices to heal from the inside out.

However, your healing journey isn't over yet. For as long as you suffer from those negative thoughts and seek external validation, you'll struggle to become the happiest, healthiest, and most vibrant version of yourself.

That's why I'd like to revisit the topic of negative thoughts before we go and share some powerful self-love practices that can help you stay on the right path on a daily basis. By using EFT tapping, mirror work, and journaling, you can start living the life you want to live. Let's jump straight in.

Stopping those negative thoughts

In earlier chapters of this book, I spent time explaining how obsessive negative thought patterns can trigger or worsen your symptoms of BDD, and I shared a few tips to help you create the right environment to help you regain control

However, speaking from experience, I know that this is easier said than done. You can have all the insight in the world, but unless you have tools to help you deal with these thoughts daily, you could fall back into the same unhealthy thinking patterns.

You've come a long way since then and hopefully, you've put into practice some or many of the tools that I've suggested throughout this book.

Now I want to give you three more tools that you can practice daily to keep these thoughts in check because they can and most likely will continue to challenge you. These tools are journaling, mirror work, and EFT tapping.

Remember that your inner voice is there to help and protect you from perceived threats so blocking it out can be difficult. But by listening to this voice yet detaching ourselves from it (see Chapter 6 for a recap) we can learn to heal.

Journaling

Journaling is a powerful practice that can help you give a name to your negative thoughts, get to the root of the problem, and help you understand what is going on in your mind so you can start to address it. It can also help you track your progress and identify your triggers so you can develop even more effective tools that will help you during the healing process.

By picking up a pen and paper, we are reconnecting with both our conscious and subconscious selves and understanding that these thoughts are separate from ourselves and can be shaped. Perhaps our triggers come from an insecurity we've been sitting on for a long time, someone or something from our past, or something we fear. Journaling can help unpack all of this.

Although I've never been much of a writer, I found that starting a journaling practice, or more specifically, a 'mind dump journaling practice,' was a great judgment-free space where I could let those negative thoughts flow.

How to do it

1. Grab a journal or notebook and a pen and find a quiet space where you won't be disturbed.

2. Think about how you're feeling and start to write about it. Don't feel like you have to be careful of spelling or grammar; just write down anything that comes to mind. You want to offload all those negative thoughts and emotions.

3. Be mindful of what emerges. Often, you'll see a pattern as you start to write and notice the reasons why you feel like this. Don't worry if it doesn't happen. Just keep on writing. The act itself is very therapeutic.

4. Next, tear out the page and destroy it however you like. This important step will help you release these thoughts and emotions and ensure you won't dwell on them in the future.

Ideally, make journaling part of your daily routine. I like to do mine first thing in the morning when I'm feeling most vulnerable, but you can do it whenever it works best for you. Feel free to experiment and notice the benefits.

Mirror work

You should also make mirror work a part of your daily practice, using three positive affirmations to help reinforce your strength and keep those negative thoughts quieter.

Yes, the thought of looking at yourself in the mirror may trigger uncomfortable thoughts and feelings but it's often exactly what you need to move forward.

By doing so, you'll start to overcome your inner critic, cultivate self-compassion, self-love, and acceptance, and start to break the association you have between the mirror and those obsessive negative thoughts about your appearance.

When I first started to do this, I felt beyond uncomfortable. I'd spent many years criticizing my appearance in a mirror. Flipping this habit definitely pushed me out of my comfort zone.

But as I followed my self-defined 90-day mirror work goal, I noticed that it did start to get better. My negative thoughts were slowly replaced by positive ones as I started to believe the affirmations I was repeating.

This is exactly what I want you to do. Set yourself a goal of 90 days, then start your mirror work practice by doing the following:

1. Choose three self-love affirmations from the following list:[36]

- I love my body and I love myself.

- I am perfect and complete just the way I am.

- I feed my body healthy, nourishing food and give it healthy, nourishing exercise because it deserves to be taken care of.

- I know the answers and solutions. I listen to myself and trust my inner judgment.

- My brain is my sexiest body part.

- My life is what I make of it. I have all the power.

- My body is a vessel for my awesomeness.

- Being grounded and whole makes me beautiful. I can get there just by being still, breathing, listening to my intuition, and doing what I can to be kind to myself and others.

- I deserve to be treated with love and respect.

- Even if I don't see how amazing I am, there is someone who does. I am loved and admired.

- I look exactly the way I'm supposed to. I know because this is the way God (use whatever religious or spiritual higher power you believe in made me!

2. Write these three self-love affirmations on Post-it notes and stick them to your chosen mirror.

---

[36]   45 positive affirmations to improve your body image. 80 Twenty Nutrition. (2018, May 7). Retrieved March 30, 2023, from https://80twentynutrition.com/blog/nutrition-news/positive-affirmations-to-improve-your-body-image/

3. Put on some calming music and look at your face in the mirror for five minutes. Use your breath to be present and feel calm.

4. Repeat your chosen affirmations, feeling their positivity and truth in every cell of your body.

That's it! Make a note in your diary or calendar when the 90 days are up, then mark off your progress every day. I love using my phone calendar for this as it really helps me to keep track.

Even when your 90-day challenge is over, repeat your mirror work as often as you can. You can even increase it to ten minutes if you feel that this practice is making a big difference to your life and body image.

EFT Tapping for beginners

Have you heard of EFT (Emotional Freedom Technique)? It's a form of energy healing that stimulates acupressure and meridian points to restore our energy balance and relieve negative thoughts, feelings, and beliefs.[37]

Similar to acupuncture (but without the needles), it can have various benefits, including reducing stress and pain, breaking bad habits, easing depression and anxiety, and helping with PTSD and trauma.

As you tap your body, you'll start to release memories that could have triggered your negative thoughts, such as the school bully who teased you about the shape of your ears. Then you can start to overcome this thought or memory and move forward with your life

What I love about the technique is the fact that it can be used anytime and in any place. It helps me feel more in control of my health and healing because I can soothe myself without turning to those old obsessive behaviors.

How to use EFT for BDD in 3 easy steps

EFT is divided into five key steps that should be followed in turn to focus on a particular negative thought or problem. If you have more than this, feel free to repeat as desired. Here's how to do it.

---

[37]   Anthony, K. (2023, February 1). What is EFT tapping? 5-step technique for anxiety relief. Healthline. Retrieved March 30, 2023, from https://www.healthline.com/health/eft-tapping#What-is-EFT-tapping

1. Identify the issue

Decide which painful memory or emotion is causing you problems then come up with a short phrase to refer to it, such as "I'm struggling with my body image".

2. Create a set-up statement

Once you've done this, create an affirmation based on the problem. For example, "Even though I'm struggling with my body image, I deeply and profoundly love and accept myself."

3. Start EFT tapping

Finally, you can start tapping on the ends of the five meridian points, repeating the phrase you outlined above, in step three. Stay focused on the feeling as you do so. The points you should cover are:

- Eyebrow (EB). Where the eyebrows start at the bridge of the nose.

- Side of the eye (SE). On the bone along the outside of either eye.

- Under the eye (UE). On the top of the cheekbone under either eye.

- Under the nose (UN). The area beneath the nose and above the upper lip.

- Chin point (Ch). The crease between your bottom lip and chin.

- Collarbone point (CB). About two inches below and to the side of where your collar bones meet.

- Under the arm (UA). On each side, about four inches beneath the armpits.

- Top of the head (TOH). Directly on the crown of your head.

- Karate chop (KC). The outer edge of the hand, on the opposite side from the thumb.

I understand that learning these points from a book can be tricky. That's why I recommend you see an EFT practitioner first or watch the excellent YouTube video 'How to Tap with Jessica Ortner'.[38]

How to stop comparing yourself to others and focus on yourself

Comparing ourselves to others is a natural human habit that can help inspire us to achieve more and put our best foot forward in life. For example, we might meet someone with admirable language skills and feel motivated to take classes so we can also reach these impressive levels.

But more often than not, they can fuel our body image issues and insecurities, feeding that negative inner voice and leaving us feeling overwhelmed with our perceived failures. In this age of social media and airbrushed or filtered images, we can't help but feel that something is wrong with us.

If we continue to compare ourselves to others, we can hold back our healing and get stuck in that place of suffering and pain.

We already mentioned how to create a positive environment for yourself in earlier chapters, but now I want to give you more tips on how to stop comparing yourself every day.

1. Become aware of your triggers

Think about yourself for a moment now. Who have you compared yourself to in the last 24 hours? Did you feel like your appearance and life paled in comparison? Did it trigger feelings of failure and inadequacy inside? Social media is often the biggest offender.

2. Avoid your triggers

Use this information to write a list of your most usual triggers. You can then use this to avoid them as much as possible. For example, you may want to avoid social media for a while or limit your time spent online. Or perhaps there's a particular friend or activity that ignited these feelings inside. How could you avoid them in the future?

3. Become your own best friend

How do you speak to a friend who's in the middle of a crisis? Most likely, you don't speak to yourself the same way.

---

[38] YouTube. (2013, April 11). How to tap with Jessica Ortner: Emotional freedom technique informational video. YouTube. Retrieved March 30, 2023, from https://www.youtube.com/watch?v=pAclBdj20ZU

Instead, you probably criticize yourself and allow that inner negative voice to control the dialogue. I want you to break this cycle and instead foster kindness, self-love, and self-compassion.

4. Start a gratitude journal

Take a few moments each day to write down ten things you're grateful for. By doing this, you'll start to appreciate the beauty and positivity in your life. Whenever you're feeling low, you can refer back to your list and boost your mood.

5. Remind yourself that other people's 'outsides' can't be compared to your 'insides'

Often we believe that people's appearances represent their outside world. But the truth is, people who appear to be happy and have everything together are often battling their own demons. Remember that you don't know what goes on behind closed doors.

6. Stop seeking validation and let go of the need for approval

When we compare ourselves to others, we believe that we need to be exactly like them if we are to be validated and approved. Not only does this trigger those negative thoughts but it can also hold us back in life. Instead, keep building your sense of self and focus on your unique value. Go back and review the section on setting boundaries in Chapter 4 if you need more help.

Summary

By reading through this chapter, you've learned a range of self-love tools that will be there to support you when you feel emotionally challenged or overwhelmed, including EFT tapping, mirror work, and journaling. You'll also see the value in self-love and just how harmful it is for you to compare yourself to others.

Conclusion

Congratulations on making it to the end of this book! I know that so many people (me included) dream about living an incredible and fulfilling life, but give up because they believe that it's too difficult, that they will never heal, or that they don't deserve to feel good.

You are different.

You've shown your inner resolve, strength, and willingness to break out from the clutches of BDD, no matter how challenging it may feel. This shows that you, too, can heal. Of course, this is going to take time.

Just as these negative thoughts and feelings about yourself and the world took time to take root, it will also take time to nurture yourself and prune away the overgrowth so you can emerge like a butterfly from the chrysalis. As Anita Moorjani said, "Love yourself like your life depends on it because it does."

Simply start small, take those baby steps in the right direction and you will be able to live the life you want and deserve. Healing isn't a race and there are no time constraints. Nor is it linear.

However, I promise, over time, you can break free from BDD.

You deserve to be authentically you and live the life of your dreams. So don't give up on yourself. Seek help if you need it, be patient, follow the practices I shared in this book, and you can get there.

Thank you!

Before I leave you, I want to thank you for reading this book and allowing me to share my own experience of BDD with you and the story of my healing journey. Although there are still moments when I feel challenged by the world or notice that my thoughts are spiraling once again, I now have the tools to stop it in its tracks and quickly prevent myself from suffering as intensely as I once did.

If you've loved this book, please go ahead and leave me a five-star rating on Amazon then share it with someone else who you know needs to hear my words. Together, we can change the world and help others to overcome BDD and enjoy a rich and fulfilling life.

Thank You

Inner healing is my passion, thank you for your support in purchasing this Ebook. I commend you on taking the steps toward accepting, respecting and loving yourself inside and out. You deserve to feel happy and whole.
If you would please leave me an honest review of your thoughts, I would greatly appreciate it.

-Caldwell Ramsey

References

PG 12. Cleveland Clinic. (n.d.). Body dysmorphic disorder (BDD): Symptoms & treatment. Cleveland Clinic. Retrieved March 4, 2023, from https://my.clevelandclinic.org/health/diseases/9888-body-dysmorphic-disorder#

PG 16. Veale, D., Ellison, N., Werner, T., Dodhia, R., Serfaty, M., & Clarke, A. (n.d.). Do I have BDD? Take the test. BDDF. Retrieved March 3, 2023, from https://bddfoundation.org/information/do-i-have-bdd-test/

OCD Foundation. (n.d.). Subtypes of BDD. BDD. Retrieved March 3, 2023, from https://bdd.iocdf.org/about-bdd/subtypes-of-bdd/

PG 20. Deshpande, R., Lai, T. M., Li, W., & Feusner, J. (n.d.). The neurobiology of body dysmorphic disorder. BDD. Retrieved March 3, 2023, from https://bdd.iocdf.org/professionals/neurobiology-of-bdd/

PG 22. BDD Foundation. (n.d.). Feeling suicidal? BDDF. Retrieved March 3, 2023, from https://bddfoundation.org/support/feeling-suicidal/

PG 25. BDD Foundation . (n.d.). Famous people with BDD. BDDF. Retrieved March 13, 2023, from https://bddfoundation.org/information/more-about-bdd/famous-people-with-bdd/

PG 26. Abed, R. T. (n.d.). An Evolutionary Hypothesis For Obsessive

Compulsive Disorder: A Psychological Immune System? An evolutionary hypothesis for obsessive compulsive disorder: A psychological immune system? Retrieved March 13, 2023, from https://web-archive.southampton.ac.uk/cogprints.org/1147/1/ocd-final.htm

PG. 27 Causes of body dysmorphic disorder (BDD). Mind.org. (2022, July). Retrieved March 14, 2023, from https://www.mind.org.uk/information-support/types-of-mental-health-problems/body-dysmorphic-disorder-bdd/causes/

Amen, D. (2017, September 1). Can ostracism cause lingering pain in your brain? Amen Clinics Can Ostracism Cause Lingering Pain in Your Brain Comments. Retrieved March 13, 2023, from https://www.amenclinics.com/blog/ostracism-causes-lingering-pain-in-the-brain-2/

PG. 28 What causes BDD? BDDF. (n.d.). Retrieved March 14, 2023, from https://bddfoundation.org/information/frequently-asked-questions/what-causes-bdd/\

PG 34.

Mindsets: Definition, examples, and books (growth, fixed + other types). The Berkeley Well-Being Institute. (n.d.). Retrieved March 14, 2023, from https://www.berkeleywellbeing.com/mindsets.html

PG 38.

The LEADERSHAPE Institute. Boise State University. (2022, May). Retrieved March 14, 2023, from https://www.boisestate.edu/getinvolved/lead/leadershape/

PG 41. Rohn, J. (n.d.). You're the average of the five people you spend the most time with. Business Insider. Retrieved March 14, 2023, from https://www.businessinsider.com/jim-rohn-youre-the-average-of-the-five-people-you-spend-the-most-time-with-2012-7

PG. 43. https://www.amazon.com/Heal-Your-Body-Louise-Hay/dp/0937611352

PG. 58 Cherry, K. (2021, June 27). What is a mood tracker? Verywell Mind. Retrieved March 20, 2023, from https://www.verywellmind.com/what-is-a-mood-tracker-5119337

PG. 60 Cherry, K. (2021, October 29). What is gratitude? Verywell Mind. Retrieved March 20, 2023, from https://www.verywellmind.com/what-is-gratitude-5206817

PG. 61 Joshua Brown Joshua Brown, Brown, J. B. J., & Wong, J. W. J. (n.d.). How gratitude changes you and your brain. Greater Good. Retrieved March 20, 2023, from https://greatergood.berkeley.edu/article/item/how_gratitude_changes_you_and_your_brain

PG. 63 Tolle, E., & Tolle, E. (2016). Practicing the power of now: Essential teachings, meditations, and exercises from the power of now. Amazon. Retrieved March 20, 2023, from https://www.amazon.com/Power-Now-Eckhart-Tolle/dp/B0095GVWMA

What is self-esteem? Mind. (n.d.). Retrieved March 20, 2023, from https://www.mind.org.uk/information-support/types-of-mental-health-problems/self-esteem/about-self-esteem/

"Am I ok today?" - BDD and the role of self-esteem. BDD. (n.d.). Retrieved March 20, 2023, from https://bdd.iocdf.org/expert-opinions/am-i-ok-today-bdd-and-the-role-of-self-esteem/

PG. 66 Lucile Hernandez Rodriguez. (2022, November 11). 20 positive self love affirmations you'll want to do daily. Lucile Hernandez Rodriguez. Retrieved March 20, 2023, from https://www.lucilehr.com/blog/positive-self-love-affirmations-youll-want-to-do-daily

PG. 67 Create a healthy nervous system and thrive no matter what. Mastin Kipp. (2022, December 19). Retrieved March 20, 2023, from https://mastinkipp.com/

PG. 68 https://www.div12.org/wp-content/uploads/2015/06/Valued-Living-Questionnaire.pdf

https://datadatabase.files.wordpress.com/2011/03/schwartz-value-inventory.pdf

https://survey.valuescentre.com/ survey.

Made in the USA
Middletown, DE
30 October 2023

41636363R00071